THE

EVERYTHING®

Wedding

ORGANIZER

5TH EDITION

Welcome to the EVERYTHING. Series!

These handy, accessible books give you all you
need to tackle a difficult project, gain a new hobby,
or even brush up on something you learned back in
school but have since forgotten.

When you're done reading, you can finally
say you know **EVERYTHING®**!

PUBLISHER Karen Cooper

MANAGING EDITOR, EVERYTHING® SERIES Lisa Laing

COPY CHIEF Casey Ebert

ASSISTANT PRODUCTION EDITOR Jo-Anne Duhamel

ACQUISITIONS EDITOR Lisa Laing

SENIOR DEVELOPMENT EDITOR Brett Palana-Shanahan

EVERYTHING® SERIES COVER DESIGNER Erin Alexander

Visit the entire Everything® series at www.everything.com

THE

EVERYTHING®

Wedding

ORGANIZER

5TH EDITION

CHECKLISTS, CHARTS, & WORKSHEETS FOR

Planning the Perfect Day!

SHELLY HAGEN

Aadamsmedia
Avon, Massachusetts

Contents

Chapter 8 ❧ Style for the Aisle / 108

Chapter 9 ❧ The Ins and Outs of Receptions / 127

Chapter 10 ❧ Food, Glorious (Catered) Food / 148

Chapter 14 ✣ Flowers and Floral Design / 226

Chapter 15 ✣ Let Them Eat Cake! / 244

Chapter 16 ✣ Getting There / 254

Chapter 17 ❧ Little Legalities / 270

Chapter 18 ❧ The Rehearsal / 282

Chapter 19 ❧ Your Honeymoon and Beyond / 294

CHAPTER 1

Begin with a Plan

THE MOMENT YOU'VE WAITED FOR, dreamed of, counted on has finally arrived—you've got the ring and you're on your way to Happily Ever After . . . right after you settle the little matter of the wedding. If you're like most brides these days, you'll have a regular arsenal of information to rely on, from your close friends to bridal publications to the good old Internet. You could also be bombarded by well-meaning advisors. Just remember that planning the big day is a very individual thing, and when it comes to making the decisions, the only opinion that matters is yours (and your fiancé's, of course).

We Have Some News!

There are several ways to share your exciting news with friends, family, and your community. One easy and time-tested way to spread the word is through a newspaper announcement. This announcement is usually made by the parents of the bride. Typically, the newspaper announcement provides general information about the bride and groom, their schooling, careers, and so on. Many couples include an official engagement photo along with the announcement. Keep in mind that some newspapers charge a fee for this service.

You may also want to set up your own engagement/wedding website, which is great for blogging about your engagement story, sharing wedding-planning updates, posting save-the-date announcements, uploading pictures of you and your sweetie, providing info about your shower and registries, and just generally creating a community feel to your upcoming wedding. There are plenty of low-cost and even free wedding site template companies online—a simple Internet search will provide you with an array of choices to begin creating and sharing instantly.

Another thing to consider is a photo shoot. Couples today are hiring professional photographers to capture the joy of the engagement, often in casual, outdoorsy settings. These pictures are often used in save-the-date mailings or postings.

Choosing the Date

As soon as you start flashing that ring around, friends and family will have two sure-bet responses:

1. "It's GORGEOUS! [Fiancé] did a great job picking it out!"
2. "So, when's the big day?"

NEWSPAPER ANNOUNCEMENT WORKSHEET

To appear in   newspaper on   (date).
....

Names of the bride's parents:
....

....

....

Address:
....

....

....

Telephone number with area code:
....

Mr. and Mrs.   of   announce the
....
          (bride's parents' names)   *(their city, if out of town)*

engagement of their daughter,   , to   ,
....
         (bride's first and middle names)   *(groom's first and last names)*

the son of Mr. and Mrs.   , of   .
....
        (groom's parents' names)   *(groom's parents' city)*

A   wedding is planned. (Or, No date has been set for the wedding.)
....
(month/season)

Some couples have already discussed the particulars of the nuptials before the engagement ring makes its way onto the bride's finger, so you might already have an answer ready to roll. But many couples want to just revel in the beauty of their newly minted engaged status before they get down to planning, and that's fine. Just be aware that event planning takes time and coordination of many services, so don't expect to start planning in April and pull off a wedding on a Saturday in June for 200 guests—unless you're shooting for June of the following year.

Couples these days tend to plan their weddings based on finances and realistic expectations. Many live together already, so it's not as though they're champing at the bit to begin their life together—the wedding is the legal culmination of the relationship they already have, not a societal blessing for them to share a bedroom. As a result, many engaged couples take their time to secure the wedding locations and/or vendors they want at a price they can afford, since most couples are also paying for a significant portion of the wedding these days.

Financial Considerations

If you're like most couples, cost will figure into your decision about when to have your wedding. Know that spring, summer, and fall dates are usually booked well in advance, since each of these seasons offers its own special air of wedding wonderment. You can also expect to pay a premium for wedding services at those times of the year, while vendors might be more willing to haggle during their downtimes. Finding a reception hall and a baker in the Northeast in the dead of winter (January through March), for example, usually doesn't require as much lead-time and could save you some cash.

If you're going bargain-hunting, you can always begin by asking an event hall if they've had any cancellations. One bride lucked out when a couple called off their wedding and left a

Saturday in September wide open. She and her now husband got a deal on almost everything—the rental fee, the catering, even the flowers. The couple had to pull everything else together (a band, a cake, a dress) in about two months' time, but they also saved about $10,000, and since both families were local, there were virtually no travel arrangements to worry about.

Happy Holidays

When guests are coming from all around the country, couples sometimes try to plan their wedding around a holiday, when folks might have some time off from work. There are pros and cons to this approach: On the positive side, people may appreciate a wedding on a long weekend; it gives them an extra day to recuperate from the festivities or to travel. For you and your fiancé, taking your honeymoon during a holiday week may give you an extra day away.

However, what if your guests already have long-weekend vacation plans? This is where problems may arise. Some people, for instance, may not be able to attend a wedding scheduled for the Friday after Thanksgiving because they are visiting family who live out of town. On the other hand, your out-of-town relatives might appreciate the convenience of a single trip combining both the holiday and the wedding.

A wedding during the Christmas season can be a beautiful and spiritual experience, but it can also be very hectic for you, your attendants, and your guests. Not only will you need to plan a wedding, but you will also need to finish your shopping, wrapping, cooking, and other projects in time for the holiday, too. All of these activities can add up to an overwhelming wedding week!

If you and/or your betrothed is Jewish, there are certain religious restrictions that make choosing a date even more challenging. Weddings are not permitted on the Sabbath (Friday evening to Saturday one half hour after sundown) or the major holidays (Rosh Hashanah, Yom Kippur, Passover, Shavuot, and

Succoth), so keep that in mind, as well. Even if you don't adhere to these restrictions, your relatives may.

Choosing a Destination Wedding

Destination weddings are very popular these days. People tend to have mixed feelings on these events, depending on how well they know the couple, how much vacation time they have, and how much money they have to spend on travel. Just be aware that even if close friends turn down an invite to your island nuptials, they wish you well.

The most popular locales for destination weddings include the Caribbean, Hawaii, cruise ships, the Virgin Islands (U.S. and British), the wine countries of California and New York State, and beaches up and down the East and West Coasts. (Las Vegas also makes the list, although it's unclear if these are elopements or planned ceremonies.) However, by definition, destination weddings can take place anywhere, so if St. Louis holds a special place in your heart, there's no reason you can't plan a wedding there. Generally speaking, though, guests may be more excited to attend a destination wedding that feels like a vacation for them.

The Budget

After you decide on the type of wedding, you'll need to figure out exactly how you're going to pay for it. The amount you allocate will help you determine the number of guests you can invite, the location of your reception, the food you choose, the number of photographs you will have taken, the type and number of flowers and centerpieces, and, really, just about every other element of the celebration.

There are two ways of setting a budget. The first is to determine the amount of money that's available right now. This will include any money that you and your fiancé may have squirreled away for the event, as well as any contributions (from your parents, for example) that you're expecting. The total amount of these resources is your budget—assuming that you're planning to pay cash for the bulk of your wedding expenses.

Another way to go about this—especially if you're pretty sure your parents will want to chip in to defray your costs, but you're unsure of how generous they plan on being—is to try tallying up the cost of your ideal wedding before asking for financial assistance. You may find that you'll get a better response if you have an estimate to present to your backers, rather than just asking for a contribution. The Wedding Budget Worksheet will be a valuable resource to you in this regard, because it will give you a good idea of how much services and items in an average wedding cost.

You'll need to do your homework. If you have friends who have been married recently, don't be shy about asking them how much they paid for things. Most newlyweds are happy to pass on the wisdom they gained from going through the wedding-planning experience themselves.

Once you've consulted your friends, pick up the phone. Call several reception sites and caterers and ask for their wedding menus to get an estimate of the per-person rates. Be sure to ask about any additional fees they may charge (such as rental fees, set-up fees, gratuity, corkage, or cake-cutting fees). Do the same with photographers, limousine services, videographers, and so on.

Once you have the estimates, you can insert cost ranges into the Wedding Budget Worksheet to give you a "cheapest to costliest" scenario. Then you can find the average price of each item and figure out which services are most important to you. Maybe it's more important for you to have a top-of-the-line photographer and just a fairly average cake (or vice-versa!). That's using your noggin to figure out where your wedding dollars are best spent.

Traditional Expenses

It is customary for the bride's family to pay the majority of the wedding expenses, but this tradition harkens back to the days where brides married young, they certainly weren't working outside of the home, and weddings didn't cost a small fortune. These days, many brides and grooms bear the brunt of the wedding expenses themselves. If the idea of paying for your own wedding sends your head spinning, keep in mind that your own opinions carry more weight if *you* are the one writing the checks. The opposite holds true if you accept contributions from your parents. If you're spending their money, you'll want (or will be encouraged by them) to carefully consider all of their suggestions, too.

The bride and her family traditionally pay for the following:

* The groom's wedding ring
* Gift for the groom
* Invitations, reception cards, and announcements
* The bride's wedding gown and accessories
* Fee for ceremony location
* Decorative flowers for ceremony and reception (including flowers for bridesmaids)
* Photography
* Music for ceremony and reception
* Reception costs (location rental, food, decorations, and so on)

Other expenses can include rented transportation, such as limousines, accommodations for bridesmaids, and gifts for bridesmaids.

WEDDING BUDGET WORKSHEET

Item	Projected Cost*	Deposit Paid	Balance Due	Who Pays?
WEDDING CONSULTANT				
Fee				
Tip *(usually 15–20%)*				
PREWEDDING PARTIES				
Engagement (if hosted by bride and groom)				
Site rental				
Equipment rental				
Invitations				
Food				
Beverages				
Decorations				
Flowers				
Party favors				
Bridesmaids' party/luncheon				
Rehearsal dinner (if hosted by bride and groom)				
Site rental				
Equipment rental				
Invitations				
Food				
Beverages				
Decorations				
Flowers				
Party favors				

Including tax, if applicable

Item	Projected Cost*	Deposit Paid	Balance Due	Who Pays?
CEREMONY				
Location fee				
Officiant's fee				
Donation to church *(optional, amount varies)*				
Organist/on-site musician				
Tip *(amount varies)*				
Other musicians				
Tip *(amount varies)*				
Program				
Aisle runner				
BUSINESS AND LEGAL MATTERS				
Marriage license				
Blood test *(if applicable)*				
WEDDING JEWELRY				
Engagement ring				
Bride's wedding band				
Groom's wedding band				
BRIDE'S FORMALWEAR				
Wedding gown				
Alterations				
Undergarments *(slip, bustier, hosiery, etc.)*				
Headpiece				
Shoes				

Including tax, if applicable

Item	Projected Cost*	Deposit Paid	Balance Due	Who Pays?
BRIDE'S FORMALWEAR *(continued)*				
Jewelry *(excluding engagement and wedding rings)*				
Purse *(optional)*				
Cosmetics, or makeup stylist				
Hairstylist				
Going-away accessories				
Honeymoon clothes				
GROOM'S FORMALWEAR				
Tuxedo				
Shoes				
Honeymoon clothes				
GIFTS				
Bride's attendants				
Groom's attendants				
Bride *(optional)*				
Groom *(optional)*				
RECEPTION				
Site rental				
Equipment rental *(chairs, tent, etc.)*				
Decorations				
Servers, bartenders				

Including tax, if applicable

Item	Projected Cost*	Deposit Paid	Balance Due	Who Pays?
RECEPTION (continued)				
Wine service for cocktail hour				
Hors d'oeuvres				
Entrées				
Meals for hired help				
Nonalcoholic beverages				
Wine				
Champagne				
Liquor				
Dessert				
Toasting glasses				
Guest book				
Place cards				
Printed napkins				
Party favors				
Box or pouch for envelope gifts				
Tip for caterer or banquet manager *(usually 15–20%)*				
Tip for servers, bartenders *(usually 15–20% total)*				
PHOTOGRAPHY AND VIDEOGRAPHY				
Engagement portrait				
Wedding portrait				
Wedding proofs				

Including tax, if applicable

Item	Projected Cost*	Deposit Paid	Balance Due	Who Pays?
PHOTOGRAPHY AND VIDEOGRAPHY *(continued)*				
Photographer's fee				
Album				
Mothers' albums				
Extra prints				
Videographer's fee				
RECEPTION MUSIC				
Musicians for cocktail hour				
Tip *(optional, up to 15%)*				
Live band				
Tip *(optional, usually $25 per band member)*				
Disc jockey				
Tip *(optional, usually 15–20%)*				
FLOWERS AND DECORATIONS				
Flowers for wedding site				
Decorations for wedding site				
Bride's bouquet				
Bridesmaids' flowers				
Boutonnieres				
Corsages				
Flowers for reception site				
Potted plants				

*Including tax, if applicable

Item	Projected Cost*	Deposit Paid	Balance Due	Who Pays?
FLOWERS AND DECORATIONS *(continued)*				
Table centerpieces				
Head table				
Cake table				
Decorations for reception				
WEDDING INVITATIONS AND STATIONERY				
Invitations				
Announcements/Save the date				
Thank-you notes				
Calligrapher				
Postage *(for invitations and response cards)*				
WEDDING CAKE				
Wedding cake				
Groom's cake				
Cake top and decorations				
Flowers for cake				
Cake serving set				
Cake/dessert boxes				
WEDDING TRANSPORTATION				
Limousines or rented cars				
Parking				
Tip for drivers *(usually 15–20%)*				

Including tax, if applicable

WEDDING BUDGET WORKSHEET (CONTINUED)

Item	Projected Cost*	Deposit Paid	Balance Due	Who Pays?
GUEST ACCOMMODATIONS				
Guest transportation				
HONEYMOON				
Transportation				
Accommodations				
Meals				
Spending money				
ADDITIONAL EXPENSES (LIST BELOW)				
Total of All Expenses				

*Including tax, if applicable

The groom and his family are traditionally responsible for the following expenses:

- The bride's wedding and engagement rings
- Gift for the bride
- Marriage license
- Officiant's fee
- The bride's bouquet, mothers' and grandmothers' corsages, boutonnieres for groomsmen
- Rehearsal dinner
- Honeymoon

His family also may opt to pay for the groomsmen's lodging.

Wedding Planners: Pros, Cons, and Costs

Some couples choose to employ a wedding planner to help them coordinate the many details of the big event. Wedding planners (or consultants) have extensive knowledge, ideas, and contacts you might not have even thought of. Not everyone needs or wants a planner, and you shouldn't feel you have to hire one just because someone else did. Some couples enjoy planning their own weddings and have plenty of time to do so. However, you may find that a consultant can relieve a great deal of the planning pressure you are facing, especially if you're short on time because of work obligations, or tend to feel overwhelmed when planning a big project.

Once you find someone you might be interested in working with, schedule an appointment with her. Here are some questions to ask:

- How long has she been in business?
- Is she a full-time or a part-time consultant?

WEDDING PLANNER WORKSHEET

Name:
....

Address:
....

Website:
....

Phone:
....

Contact:
....

Hours:
....

APPOINTMENTS

Date: Time:
....

Date: Time:
....

Date: Time:
....

Date: Time:
....

SERVICE

Number of hours:
....

Overtime cost:
....

Provides the following services:
....

....

....

....

....

....

COST

Fee: ◯ Flat ◯ Hourly ◯ Percentage _____ ◯ Per guest

Total amount due:

Amount of deposit: Date:

Amount due: Date:

Gratuities included? ◯ Yes ◯ No

Sales tax included? ◯ Yes ◯ No

Date contract signed:

Terms of cancellation:

Notes:

- Does she have references?
- How many weddings does she plan in a typical month? On a typical weekend?
- What is the cost, and how will you pay? (Hourly? Flat fee? Percentage?)
- What services are included in her quoted price?

The consultant you choose may offer different levels of service. She may give you the option of hiring her to help you plan the entire event down to the tiniest detail or simply using her services for scoping out reception locations and caterers.

Don't forget to check references. This is your one chance to get this day just the way you want it, so be sure she gives you the names of a few other brides who've used her services recently. Call and ask them to elaborate on their experience with her: what was fabulous; what didn't go according to plan; how the consultant handled any last-minute surprises, etc.

The cost of a wedding consultant will vary, depending on the type and extent of service you require. Some will bill between 10 and 20 percent of the total cost of the wedding, while others will charge a flat fee. Resort- and hotel-affiliated consultants, on the other hand, are usually at your service at no extra charge, if you are already doing business with their employer.

Wedding planners are all the rage on bridal reality TV shows, and they do provide a very valuable service—particularly those planners who allow you to customize your level of service with them. However, if you have a little dedication, some negotiating skills, and a mom, sister, friend, or fiancé who really wants to help, you can definitely plan your wedding by yourself. And this book can serve as your ultra-affordable wedding consultant during that time.

Prewedding Checklist

Many of the following tasks may be (and should be) attended to in the days just before your wedding. Try to accomplish them up to a week ahead of time. Then, you can relax and enjoy your last week of single life!

Planning Checklist

Six to twelve months before the wedding:
O Decide on type of wedding.
O Decide on time of day.
O Choose the location.
O Set a date.
O Set a budget.
O Select bridal party.
O Plan color scheme.
O Select and order bridal gown.
O Select and order headpiece.
O Select and order shoes.
O Select and order attendants' gowns.
O Start honeymoon planning.
O Go to bridal gift registry.
O Start compiling the guest list.
O Select caterer.
O Select band or DJ.
O Select florist.
O Select photographer/videographer.
O Start planning reception.
O Reserve hall, hotel, etc., for reception.
O Attend premarital counseling at your church, if applicable.
O Select and order wedding rings.
O Reserve accommodations for guests.
O Reserve formalwear for groomsmen and groom.

Three to four months before the wedding:

O Complete guest list.

O Plan to have mothers select attire.

O Select and order invitations.

O Order personal stationery.

O Start compiling trousseau (a fancy word that is used to refer to the bride's undergarments and accessories, and is now commonly used when speaking of all wedding- and honeymoon-related garments).

O Finalize reception arrangements. (Rent items such as tents, tables, chairs, and so on now.)

O Make reservations for honeymoon.

O Confirm dress delivery.

O Confirm time and date with florist.

O Confirm time and date with caterer.

O Confirm time and date with photographer/videographer.

O Confirm time and date with band or DJ.

O Confirm time and date with wedding site.

O Discuss transportation to and from ceremony and reception.

O Order cake.

O Select and order attire for groomsmen.

O Schedule bridesmaids' dress and shoe fittings.

Six to eight weeks before the wedding:

O Mail all invitations to allow time for RSVPs.

O Arrange for an appointment to get marriage license.

O Finalize honeymoon arrangements.

O Schedule appointments at beauty salon for attendants.

O Schedule bridesmaids' luncheon or party.

O Plan rehearsal and rehearsal dinner.

O Schedule bridal photo shoot.

One month before the wedding:

O Begin to record gifts received and send thank-you notes.
O Send bridal portrait with announcement to newspaper.
O Purchase gifts for bridal party.
O Purchase gift for fiancé, if you are exchanging gifts.
O Schedule your final dress fitting, including accessories and shoes.
O Obtain wedding props, e.g., pillow for ringbearer, candles, etc.
O Get marriage license.

Two weeks before the wedding:

O Finalize wedding-day transportation.
O Arrange to change name on driver's license, Social Security card, etc.
O Confirm any accommodations for the guests.
O Prepare wedding announcements to be mailed after the wedding.
O Plan reception seating arrangements.

One week before the wedding:

O Start packing for your honeymoon.
O Finalize the number of guests with your caterer.
O Double-check all details with those providing professional services (photographer, videographer, florist, etc.).
O Confirm desired shots with photographer.
O Style your hair with the headpiece.
O Practice applying cosmetics in proper lighting.
O Arrange for one last fitting for all of your wedding attire.
O Make sure rings are picked up and fit properly.
O Confirm receipt of marriage license.
O Have rehearsal and rehearsal dinner (one or two days before wedding).
O Arrange to have the photographer and attendants arrive two hours before ceremony for prewedding pictures.
O Arrange for music to start thirty minutes before ceremony.
O Arrange to have mother of the groom seated five minutes before ceremony.

O Arrange to have mother of the bride seated immediately before the processional.

O Arrange for aisle runner to be rolled out by the groomsmen immediately before the processional.

O Reconfirm plans with your officiant, reception site coordinator, photographer, videographer, band or DJ, florist, baker, limousine company, and hairstylist/makeup artist. Make sure they know correct locations and times.

O Reconfirm honeymoon travel arrangements and hotel reservations.

O Reconfirm hotel reservation for your wedding night.

O Make sure wedding attendants know where they need to be and when, and remind them of any special duties they need to perform.

O Pack your going-away outfit and accessories. If you'll be changing at the reception site, put a trusted friend in charge of making sure everything arrives there safely.

O Make sure your honeymoon luggage is stored in the trunk of your "getaway car" or is sent ahead to wherever you're spending your wedding night.

O Give your wedding rings and marriage license to your honor attendants to hold until the ceremony.

O Make sure groom and best man have enough cash for tipping (your driver, bartenders, and anyone who goes above and beyond on your big day).

O Give an "emergency repair kit" (safety pins, extra hosiery, tissues, aspirin, etc.) to a trusted attendant, so you'll be better prepared to deal with the unexpected.

O Arrange for a friend to drive your car to the reception site if you intend to drive to the hotel or inn where you'll be staying that night.

On your wedding day:

O Try to relax and pamper yourself; take a long bath, have a manicure, etc.

O Eat at least one small meal.

O Have your hair and makeup done several hours before the ceremony.

O Start dressing one to two hours before the ceremony.

CHAPTER 2

Your Attendants

YOUR WEDDING PARTY can be as big—or as small—as you like. Formal weddings usually have a larger number of attendants than informal ones, but you can feel free to bend tradition here if you think it's appropriate. Brides often feel obligated to have certain people in the wedding, even if they're not that close to them. However, if you surround yourself with family members and close friends whom you can depend on, you may discover that those prewedding parties, fittings, and rehearsals will go more smoothly than you expected.

Choosing Bridesmaids and Groomsmen

Think about which of your close friends and family members you and your fiancé would really like to have in the wedding. Traditionally, there are an equal number of bridesmaids and groomsmen, but there is no reason why you have to adhere to this rule. The general guideline is one groomsman for every fifty guests, so that guests can be ushered to their ceremony seats in an orderly fashion. One concern brides often have is that every bridesmaid needs to have a partner to walk her down the aisle and someone to dance with during scheduled dances at the reception. But having a couple of extra groomsmen is no crime. They can walk with each other down the aisle, and they probably won't shed a tear over not dancing in the wedding party dance at the reception.

As soon as you figure out whom you want to include in your wedding party, ask them! Sometimes, due to monetary problems or other conflicts, one of your first choices may have to decline, and you want to make sure you have enough time to ask a replacement.

Above all else, try to select attendants who are comfortable working with others, who don't get flustered easily, and who have known you or your fiancé for a while. This is no time for surprises. If you're up front about what you expect from all of the attendants, you can keep complications to a minimum.

Attendants' Duties

Here's the good stuff—the duties that your attendants typically take on when they agree to be in your wedding. Don't just assume, though, that they automatically know. You still have to spell out what you have in mind for your friends and family. This way, you won't resent a bridesmaid for not doing something that she didn't even realize you expected of her. Here's a rundown of who does what.

Maid or Matron of Honor

The maid (single) or matron (married) of honor typically helps the bride address envelopes, records wedding gifts, shops, plans a bachelorette party, and takes care of any of the other important prewedding duties. She is also charged with arranging a bridal shower, with the help of your bridesmaids.

The maid of honor helps the bride dress for the ceremony. At the altar, she arranges the bride's dress and veil and holds the bride's bouquet during the vows. She is also a witness and signs the wedding certificate with the best man. After the ceremony, the maid of honor may stand in the receiving line. She helps the bride change clothes after the reception and takes care of the bridal gown.

Best Man

The best man organizes the bachelor party, which may be the one thing your fiancé is most interested in. After that, the best man drives the groom to the ceremony and holds the bride's ring until it's needed during the ceremony.

The best man is also in charge of giving the check to the officiant just before or after the ceremony. He may also be asked to pay the other professionals, such as the chauffeur or the wedding coordinator. If this is to be part of his duties, your fiancé (or his family) will give him the payments ahead of time, which he'll then pass on to the appropriate parties.

Bridesmaids

You're asking much of the women who agree to be your bridesmaids, so make sure they're up to the task. This is a significant financial commitment, much more so than for the groomsmen, mostly because bridesmaids pay for their own dresses, which can cost hundreds of dollars, whereas most groomsmen rent their tuxes for much less. One of the bridesmaids will keep a record of the gifts

BRIDE'S ATTENDANTS CONTACT INFO WORKSHEET

MAID/MATRON OF HONOR

Name:
....

Address:
....

E-mail/Phone:
....

Special duties:
....

BRIDESMAIDS

Name:
....

Address:
....

E-mail/Phone:
....

Special duties:
....

....

Name:
....

Address:
....

E-mail/Phone:
....

Special duties:
....

....

Name:
....

Address:
....

E-mail/Phone:
....

Special duties:
....

....

FLOWER GIRL

Name:
....

Address:
....

E-mail/Phone:
....

Special duties:
....

OTHER HONOR ATTENDANTS

Name:
....

Address:
....

E-mail/Phone:
....

Special duties:
....

....

Name:
....

Address:
....

E-mail/Phone:
....

Special duties:
....

....

Name:
....

Address:
....

E-mail/Phone:
....

Special duties:
....

....

GROOM'S ATTENDANTS CONTACT INFO WORKSHEET

BEST MAN

Name:
....
Address:
....
E-mail/Phone:
....
Special duties:
....

USHERS

Name:
....
Address:
....
E-mail/Phone:
....
Special duties:
....

....

Name:
....
Address:
....
E-mail/Phone:
....
Special duties:
....

....

Name:
....
Address:
....
E-mail/Phone:
....
Special duties:
....

....

RINGBEARER

Name:
....

Address:
....

E-mail/Phone:
....

Special duties:
....

OTHER HONOR ATTENDANTS

Name:
....

Address:
....

E-mail/Phone:
....

Special duties:
....

....

Name:
....

Address:
....

E-mail/Phone:
....

Special duties:
....

....

Name:
....

Address:
....

E-mail/Phone:
....

Special duties:
....

....

you receive at the shower and who gave what. The bridesmaids will assist you and/or the maid of honor with prewedding shopping or tasks and will help you prepare for the ceremony, and they will also likely throw you a shower and bachelorette party.

If you choose to have birdseed thrown or bubbles blown as you exit the wedding site, the bridesmaids will provide the guests with the necessary materials.

Groomsmen

Groomsmen are given a significant amount of responsibility, too. For starters, they'll rent (or purchase) their own formalwear. They'll arrive at the ceremony location early to assist with the setup and finishing touches, such as lighting candles or tying bows on reserved seating. They'll escort guests to their seats and meet, welcome, and seat guests of honor (such as grandparents). Just before the processional, one or two of your groomsmen will roll out the aisle runner. They'll oversee the transfer of the gifts to a secure location after the reception, and they'll probably decorate your getaway vehicle (hopefully in a tasteful manner).

Kids' Stuff

If you or your fiancé has younger relatives (or children of your own), you might want to let them play a part in your ceremony. Junior bridesmaids are usually between ten and fourteen years old, while flower girls are younger than that. Young boys, usually under ten years old, can be ringbearers. Other boys and girls, called trainbearers or pages, can walk behind the bride, carrying the train of her dress as she walks down the aisle.

The ringbearer precedes the flower girl in the procession (or, in the case of a shy ringbearer or flower girl, the kids can totter down the aisle side by side). He carries the rings, which can be tied with a ribbon and displayed on a satin pillow. For those of you who are worried about the ringbearer losing or eating your wedding bands, don't worry. The rings he carries could be fake and, to be doubly safe, perhaps sewn on or otherwise secured to the pillow. The best man and/or maid of honor will have the real rings.

The ringbearer's pillow is a simple little thing that you can make yourself, even if you don't have a crafty bone in your body. Go to a craft store and visit the bridal section. Choose the most inexpensive satin pillow. Since you're in the wedding section, you should be able to easily find faux wedding rings—grab a package of those. Wander over to the ribbon section and either purchase a spool or ask for a length of ribbon in a color that coordinates with your attendants' dresses. At home, tie the ribbon around the pillow, and attach the rings to the ribbon. Voilà! Done!

The flower girl is the last person down the aisle before the bride. Traditionally, she sprinkles fresh flower petals for the bride to walk on, but brides have been known to slip on the petals, so you may want to think about having her toss paper petals or carrying a pretty basket of fresh flowers.

If your flower girl's basket is coming in at what seems to be an unreasonable cost to you, simply make your own. Go to any craft store to find a suitable small basket, and fill it with wedding confetti or faux flower petals. This will cost you less than $50, and your flower girl will no doubt be happy just to be tossing something as she strolls down the aisle.

The page/trainbearer's only duty is to carry the bride's train and to help arrange it neatly. Strictly speaking, this job is only necessary if the bride has a very long train, but you may wish to have one or two trainbearers or pages even if your train is short (it's one more way to include cute kids in the wedding). Although most people assume that pages are always boys, there's nothing wrong with having a girl page.

Gifts for the Wedding Party

It's customary to show your gratitude to the wedding party by giving each member a little gift. Let everyone know you appreciate all the time, money, and aggravation they've spent helping to make your wedding day something you'll all enjoy and remember.

Gifts for the Bridesmaids

You want to properly thank the gals who have stood by you, tried on countless bridesmaid dresses, listened to you prattle on about your new pots and pans, and have generally been patient, indispensable pals. Possible gifts for your bridesmaids include:

- Jewelry (especially something that might complement their dresses for the wedding)
- A lush robe
- Perfume or high-end hair products
- Accessories for a smartphone (small speaker, a glitzy case, etc.)
- Gift certificate for a restaurant, spa, or boutique

Because bridesmaids usually wind up doing the lion's share of prewedding work (compared to the groomsmen, at least), you may want to do a little *extra* to show your appreciation. Many brides treat their bridesmaids to lunch or dinner several days before the wedding. If you're getting married in the late afternoon or evening and are feeling exceptionally calm, you can take your bridesmaids out for a nice brunch on the morning of the wedding.

Gifts for the Groomsmen

The groom is really in charge of bestowing the gifts on his family or friends in the wedding party, but it won't hurt to offer some suggestions, particularly if he's leaning toward buying each of them a case of beer. Possible (tasteful) gifts include:

- Money clip or wallet
- Cigars
- Tie
- Travel or shaving kit
- Gift certificate to a sporting goods store or restaurant
- A bottle of good wine or top-shelf liquor

Gifts for the Little Ones

Don't forget to get a little something for the children in the wedding party. Ask their parents what their kids are into, or, to make it really easy on yourself, pick up a gift certificate from a big-box store and let the little ones choose their own gifts!

Gifts for the Parents

Parents—yours and your fiancé's—are often forgotten in this whole gift-giving frenzy, though heaven knows why. Whether they're providing most of the funds for the wedding or simply lending moral support, it's a nice touch to acknowledge the people who have given you so much already (you know, life and everything).

A gift certificate for a weekend getaway (to relieve all the wedding stress) might be just the ticket. They might also enjoy a gift certificate for a nice dinner or a round of golf. Maybe they insist that you don't need to thank them; they love you and haven't for one moment thought twice about helping you plan the wedding you've always dreamed of having. Thank them anyway. Everyone likes to feel appreciated.

CHAPTER 3

The Guest List

SETTING OUT TO CREATE your guest list sounds easy enough, at least until you sit down and try to do it. Then you realize that your mother announces she's going to invite every relative she can find and all of your coworkers think they're coming. Best part—you don't have nearly enough room for everyone! The smartest strategy for addressing these problems is to hit them head-on. Don't try to ignore them or push them aside until the last minute.

Making the List

Start out by listing everyone you'd ideally like to invite. It may turn out that the total number is not that far beyond your reach. If you do end up having to shorten the list, set boundaries for your list and stick to them. In most cases the guest list is divided evenly between the two families, regardless of who is paying for what. Couples often split the list three ways: the bride's parents, the groom's parents, and the couple. Each group invites one-third of the guests.

Don't forget to include your attendants and your officiant (and his or her spouse).

The Children Question

If you've decided not to invite children, you can make this clear to parents by the fact that their children's names do not appear on the invitation. Just to be safe, however, make sure your mother (and anyone else who might be questioned) is aware of your policy.

Whatever you decide—kids of a certain age and no younger, or no children at all—everyone has to play by the same rules. You can't make an exception for your favorite cousin, who happens to be under your determined age limit. If you make one exception, it's a sure bet that other parents will ask, "What's she doing here if my little sweetie couldn't come?"

If there are children who are very special to you, consider making them part of the wedding. That way they'll be present for your big day, and you won't be offending anyone else.

The Guests' Guests

You will probably want to allow any "attached" guests to bring their significant others. It is also nice, but not necessary, to give unattached guests the opportunity to bring someone. This is especially appropriate for people who may not know many others at the wedding, because it will help them feel more comfortable.

Married guests are usually invited with their spouse. There is one exception to this rule. If you are very friendly with some of your coworkers and would like to invite them, you can include them as a group without their spouses.

Always give your attendants the option to bring a date, even if they're not involved with anyone at the time. These people have worked hard (and taken on a hefty financial burden) to be part of your wedding. Do them the courtesy of allowing them to share the day with someone special to them.

Sticky Situations

If a divorce between your parents or your fiancé's parents was amicable, be thankful. If, however, the relationship between the ex-spouses—or the resulting mixed families—is comparable to the tensions on any given reality show, you'd better map out a battle plan of your own on how to deal with the invitations.

Divorce

Do as much as you can beforehand to prevent any scenes at the wedding. This is your big day, and you don't want anything to happen that will upset or embarrass you. If you think this might be an issue, speak with the divorced set of parents openly and honestly. Request their cooperation and ask them to be on their best behavior.

With luck, they will be able to put aside their grievances for one day for your sake, but it's best to take precautions. Remind them of how much this day means to you. Divorced parents often think they're big enough to handle the situation, but find that when the moment arrives, emotion and tension get the best of them.

To be on the safe side, don't require divorced parents to interact or sit with each other. If necessary, have their tables situated as far away from each other as you can.

Stepparents and Stepchildren

In the same vein, if either one or both parents have remarried, consider yourself lucky if all the "exes" and "steps" get along. If there are tensions, they're your problem now—at least as far as your wedding is concerned.

If your mother and your stepmother are uncivil to one another, make it a priority to keep them separated. Don't seat them near each other at the wedding or reception, and don't ask them to pose for a "one big, happy family" picture. Take each woman aside before the wedding and lay down the law: There will be peace in the land on your wedding day or else. Beyond these steps, though, you must realize that your parents are adults. Expect them to act like adults. If they try to make a drama out of your wedding (threatening not to attend if the other ex-spouse attends, for instance), don't give in to the ploy.

The "Ex" Factor

Your or your fiancé's ex-spouse and ex-in-laws are usually left off the list. Even if things are very amicable, the presence of your ex-spouse might be upsetting to your new husband (and vice versa). Former mates are generally an unpleasant reminder of the past and this is a day dedicated to your future. In all but the most special cases (where everyone feels comfortable with the situation), inviting an ex usually turns out to be a bad idea.

Coworkers and Acquaintances

If you do need to cut the guest list, and you feel comfortable excluding work acquaintances, this may be the best way to go. When you're deciding which coworkers you want to invite, honestly evaluate your business relationships. Many people feel burdened by an invitation to an acquaintance's wedding. You could end up straining a relationship instead of strengthening it. Likewise, you may want to exclude your more distant relatives from the guest list. Again, be consistent. As long as your third cousins don't have to hear that your second cousins twice removed have been invited, they should understand your need to cut costs.

If a distant relative or acquaintance invited you to her wedding, this does not obligate you to invite her to yours. Most distant relatives and acquaintances will understand if you tell them that you're cutting costs by having a small affair. Tell them you'd love for them to be there, but you're having a small wedding, and it is impossible to invite everyone.

Out-of-Town Guests

Since your out-of-town guests will be traveling some distance to be with you on the big day, you should try to make things as pleasant and convenient for them as possible. Start by helping them find a place to stay. Guests pay for their own lodging (unless either the bride or groom's family offers to pick up the tab), but it is customary for you to provide enough information so that guests can make their own reservations.

Booking Blocks of Hotel Rooms

Some hotels will offer a lower rate for a group of rooms. Grouping your out-of-town guests in one hotel has several advantages:

- The group rates will be less expensive.
- They can mingle with the other guests during the downtime.
- They can carpool to and from the festivities.

GUEST ACCOMMODATIONS WORKSHEET

Be sure to give a copy of this to your mother, maid/matron of honor, and anyone else guests may contact for information about accommodations.

BLOCKS OF ROOMS RESERVED FOR WEDDING AT

Hotel:
....

Address:
....

Website:

Directions:
....

....

....

....

Approximate distance from ceremony site: Reception site:
....

Telephone:
....

Toll-free reservations number:
....

Fax number:
....

Number of single rooms reserved in block: Daily rate:
....

Number of double rooms reserved in block: Daily rate:
....

Total number of rooms reserved in block:

Date(s) reserved:
....

Cutoff/Last day reservations accepted:
....

Terms of agreement:
....

....

Payment procedure:
....

....

Notes:
....

....

....

....

OTHER NEARBY LODGINGS

Hotel:
....

Address:
....

Website:
....

Directions:
....

....

....

Approximate distance from ceremony site: Reception site:
....

Telephone:
....

Toll-free reservations number:
....

Daily room rate:
....

Notes:
....

....

Hotel:
....

Address:
....

Website:
....

Directions:
....

....

....

Approximate distance from ceremony site: Reception site:
....

Telephone:
....

Toll-free reservations number:
....

Daily room rate:
....

Notes:
....

....

....

GUEST LIST WORKSHEET

Name	Address	Telephone	RSVP Received?
1.			
2.			
3.			
4.			
5.			
6.			
7.			
8.			
9.			
10.			
11.			
12.			
13.			
14.			
15.			
16.			
17.			
18.			
19.			
20.			
21.			
22.			
23.			
24.			
25.			

GUEST LIST WORKSHEET (CONTINUED)

Name	Address	Telephone	RSVP Received?
26.			
27.			
28.			
29.			
30.			
31.			
32.			
33.			
34.			
35.			
36.			
37.			
38.			
39.			
40.			
41.			
42.			
43.			
44.			
45.			
46.			
47.			
48.			
49.			
50.			

GUEST LIST WORKSHEET (CONTINUED)

Name	Address	Telephone	RSVP Received?
51.			
52.			
53.			
54.			
55.			
56.			
57.			
58.			
59.			
60.			
61.			
62.			
63.			
64.			
65.			
66.			
67.			
68.			
69.			
70.			
71.			
72.			
73.			
74.			
75.			

GUEST LIST WORKSHEET (CONTINUED)

Name	Address	Telephone	RSVP Received?
76.			
77.			
78.			
79.			
80.			
81.			
82.			
83.			
84.			
85.			
86.			
87.			
88.			
89.			
90.			
91.			
92.			
93.			
94.			
95.			
96.			
97.			
98.			
99.			
100.			

Though grouping everyone at the same hotel is preferable, some guests may not be able to afford the hotels you choose. (You can help avoid this by choosing a middle-of-the-road place.) Others may have specific preferences—or may simply want their privacy.

Hospitality Gifts

A new trend gaining popularity is to include welcome bags for your guests as they check in to their lodgings. With folks traveling from near and far to attend your wedding, it is great to include a gift bag or basket full of treats or small gifts to say thank you and help guests enjoy their stay. These welcome totes can be tailored to your specific event and add an extra personal touch. Whether you are looking to get creative on a budget or splurge on your guests, you can make a memorable tote or basket for your special day. Here are some ideas to get you started:

- A canvas tote or decorative basket is a beautiful item your guests can reuse after the day, and they'll be reminded of your wedding each time they use it.
- Try including a note or thoughtful letter that expresses your appreciation for sharing the day with you. Stationery can tie in to the theme and colors of your wedding.
- Include a schedule of events for your guests to follow. This is particularly handy if transportation to and from the hotel will be provided, or if there are multiple events happening over the course of the weekend.
- Outdoor, beachfront, or destination wedding bags often include practical items such as small bottles of sunscreen, water, or bug spray. Ponchos or umbrellas are a must if the forecast is questionable. Fun sunglasses and folding fans are great too!
- If the region you're celebrating in is known for particular products, include samples of these treats for your guests to try.

Purchasing locally produced goods or foods benefits local businesses while pampering your out-of-town guests.

◆ Drinks (alcoholic or nonalcoholic) are a great way to set the tone for the celebrations to come, and can help guests cut down on hotel expenses.

◆ Provide some fun snacks for pre- and post-wedding gatherings. Include a range of salty and sweet treats for guests to munch on.

◆ Hangover cures are a must! Pain relief packets are always appreciated the morning after a big celebration. Bottled water, mints, and fresh fruit are the perfect accompaniment.

CHAPTER 4

It Is Better to Give . . .

NEED THEM OR NOT, you will receive many gifts when you get married. Whether your house is fully stocked already or you need everything, registering for gifts is an easy way to let people know what you really want and will use. With online registries, especially, shopping (and shipping) could not possibly be any easier. And that's why you'll be writing thank-you notes until your hand cramps.

The Gift Registry

Presents from your friends and family go a long way toward help-ing you and your fiancé set up your household. If the two of you have been living on your own (or together) for any amount of time, you may be thinking, "We have everything we need." Well, what about the things you want? What about those things you don't need every day but do need for special occasions such as dinner parties? This is the time to stock your home.

Though some of your closest friends and family members have probably already decided on the perfect gift for you, there are others who would appreciate a few hints. That's where the gift registry comes in.

Where and How to Register

Gift registry is a free service provided by many department, jewelry, gift, and specialty stores, and even travel agencies and sites. You and your fiancé spend an afternoon in the store choosing the things you want (yes, it's as fun as it sounds). When friends and family go into these stores, pulling up your registry is as easy as finding the touchscreen computer that contains the information. Many registries are also available online, as part of a store's website. Each purchase is noted on the registry to avoid duplicate gifts.

Although you can register for a few choice items at a small boutique, it's best to register with at least one "big box" store as well. Your registry will be available at the store branches in other cities and states and will appear on the store's website—all key advantages, especially for out-of-town guests.

Before registering with a store, ask about the policy on returns and exchanges—you don't want to be stuck with duplicate or damaged gifts. Make sure the store will take responsibility if you receive gifts intended for another couple, and vice versa.

A Typical Registry

Take your time and browse through the store. Items you likely want to register for include a formal dinnerware (china) pattern, a silverware pattern, glasses, pots and pans, linens, small appliances, and various other household items (measuring cups, candlestick holders, and so on).

When you decide on the styles, patterns, and colors you want, simply point the laser gun at the bar code and pull the trigger! If you're in a store without the bar-code guns, you may have to check the box next to the item and fill in the brand name and quantity in writing. And even though you may feel awkward about it, don't be afraid to ask for a few "big-ticket" items like a television or a couch. You may be helping friends or family who are looking to pool their money for such a gift. A typical registry might include:

Tableware	Linens	Cookware
◆ Fine china	◆ Sheets and	◆ Aluminum
◆ Everyday dishes	pillowcases	◆ Porcelain enamel
◆ Silverware/	◆ Towels	◆ Glass
flatware	◆ Tablecloths	◆ Copper
◆ Glassware	◆ Placemats	◆ Microwavable
	◆ Napkins	cookware

Online Gift Registries

Today brides and grooms have more options than ever before to receive gifts—and experiences—though online gift registries. Websites like Zola, Thankful, Traveler's Joy, and Honeyfund allow guests to choose from a myriad of gifts to give, from the traditional kitchen, bath, and dining options, to curated experiences and more unique contributions toward your honeymoon.

Guests can buy you dinner and drinks at the resort you plan to visit; treat you to a fun experience like snorkeling, a wine tasting, or spa treatments; or contribute to online funds that can go toward a trip abroad, your future home, or other larger-ticket items.

Online registries track shipping and exchanges for you, and some will even let you decide when you'd like your gift delivered. Because so many options can be found in just one place with these sites, not only will you find all of the brands and products your prefer, your guests will enjoy choosing from an assortment of gifts, and have more opportunity to give something personal.

Thank-You Notes

As soon as you receive a gift, you should send out a thank-you note. As hard as it will be considering the many notes you'll be writing, try to be warm and personal in all of them. Always mention the gift, and, if possible, how you and your fiancé will be using it. This small touch will prevent people from feeling that you just sent them a form letter (which, by the way, is completely unacceptable, no matter how busy you are). When sending notes for gifts you receive before the wedding, sign your maiden name. Here is an example of a thank-you note:

> *Dear Aunt Mary:*
>
> *Thank you for the lovely wine glasses; they are just what we needed to round out our bar set. Jim and I are looking forward to your visit next spring, when you can have a drink with us.*
>
> *Hannah*

The letter mentions the gift you received and how it's being used. Notice the sincerity, too.

GIFT REGISTRIES WORKSHEET

Be sure to give a copy of this to your mother, maid/matron of honor, and anyone else guests may ask about possible gift ideas.

Name of store:
....

Locations:
....

Website:
....

Toll-free mail order number:
....

Name(s) registry listed under:
....

Notes:
....

....

....

....

Name of store:
....

Locations:
....

Website:
....

Toll-free mail order number:
....

Name(s) registry listed under:
....

Notes:
....

....

....

Name of store:
....

Locations:
....

Website:
....

Toll-free mail order number:
....

Name(s) registry listed under:
....

Notes:
....

....

....

WEDDING GIFT RECORDER WORKSHEET

Name	Description of Gift	Thank-You Note Sent?

Returns and Exchanges

What if someone sends you a lamp fashioned from an old cowboy boot? Your first instinct, assuming your decorating tastes are in a completely different vein, might be to immediately throw the lamp out, sell it, or exchange it for something else. But it's not as simple as that. The people who bought you that gift did so with the best of intentions, spending a good deal of their time, energy, and money on you. Imagine how hurt they'd be if they visited your house a week after the wedding, expecting the lamp to hold a place of honor, only to find that you'd exchanged it for some napkin rings.

The best thing you can do to avoid this awkward situation is to wait until about a month after the wedding to exchange any unwanted or duplicate gifts. Some couples display all of the gifts they've received somewhere in their home in the days before the wedding; people who visit you at that time are likely to look for their gifts and even ask your opinions about them.

CHAPTER 5

Social Media and Your Wedding

EVERYWHERE YOU LOOK, everywhere you go, social media is there. And when planning your wedding, Facebook, Twitter, Pinterest, Instagram, and blogs are just the tip of the iceberg. Some couples are ready to take their wedding to the next level—sharing it all on social media. Other couples are looking to strike a balance between what to communicate and what to keep private, and some couples don't want any details shared online. Finding a way to manage the pros and cons of social media is a major part of today's wedding-planning experience. With knowledge and some preparation, you can use social media to your benefit as you plan your perfect day.

Using Social Media As You Plan

Before you go any further in your planning, you'll need to think about how social media will factor into your wedding plans. Will you use it to communicate with guests? Find vendors? Or do you want to trend on Twitter? Ten to fifteen years ago, e-mail and wedding websites were about the extent of social media any bride or groom utilized to plan their weddings. Since then, the reach of social media has grown by leaps and bounds. Social media has afforded couples many, many advantages, but it also has its pitfalls. There are numerous ways to make social media work for you and your wedding . . . you just need to sort them all out.

There are many ways to use social media to ease your planning and pass information along to friends, family, wedding party members, and vendors. For example:

Facebook

Facebook's impact and reach increases daily. Facebook has more than 1.6 billion monthly active users! What started as a simple tool for young adults to interact has become a daily staple for people of all ages. Facebook is a great way to share news with your social circles. It's also a great medium for planning: You can create group messages for all of your attendants, for example, and use it to keep everyone informed and in touch. When deciding upon vendors and resources for your wedding, you can "like" company and vendor pages to keep updated on deals, promotions, and new ideas.

Pinterest

Pinterest is a virtual online bulletin board that has revolutionized wedding planning. You create specific boards (flowers, candles, gowns, favors, etc.) and as you scan the Internet or Pinterest itself for wedding ideas, you "pin" the image with the correct URL/web address that corresponds to it. When you are ready to revisit that particular element, you know where to find it. Use these images for ideas if you plan to create your own centerpieces, for example, or show them to your vendors so they can see exactly what you have in mind.

Pinterest has become a huge resource for brides- and grooms-to-be and is a wealth of inspiration for any type of event. You can follow other pinners who have planned their own DIY affairs (and save their pins too). Boards can be dedicated to wedding style—vintage, country, boho, destination, or rustic, for example. Pinterest is a great place to preview wedding photography, find your gown, scope out venues, coordinate décor, gather shower ideas, select bridesmaid outfits, and more.

Twitter

How much can you say in 140 characters or fewer? You may be surprised at the amount of information that flows through Twitter as well as the relationships that are forged with those 140 characters. Twitter happens in real time . . . it moves fast. You can follow wedding taste-makers and style gurus, and you can create lists with particular tweeters based on what you are looking for. Twitter is also great for finding and following vendors and businesses in your area. Looking for a great baker or florist? Chances are that those in-the-know will be tweeting about the great products or services they offer.

Instagram

At one time, brides carried their cameras around with them, snapping photos at the florist, at the dressmaker, at the venue. Now things have been streamlined. With your smartphone or tablet you can take photos of all things wedding and nonwedding that inspire you or that you want to remember . . . and then you can share those ideas if you choose to. Instagram is the perfect medium for this.

Instagram is a mobile photo- and video-sharing social networking app that allows you to share your photos (either publicly or privately). You snap a photo, create some cool effects, and then post it to your Facebook, Twitter, Tumblr, or Flickr accounts to be shared with your followers and others. It is not only a fun way to keep up with family and friends, it's also a great way to instantly keep track of things you love and ideas that pique your interest, as well as follow wedding planners, vendors, photographers, crafters, or bloggers that inspire you.

Blogs

Blogs are hugely popular, and attract much attention from social media and conventional media. Blogs are ever-changing, and blogging is another great way to interact with others and document certain aspects of your planning and preparation. You may not want to post photos of yourself trying on your gown, but you may want to share a few photos of the venue or a crafty creation. You can update your wedding blog weekly (or more often) as you approach the big date. Wedding blogs are particularly helpful for gathering ideas as you plan, to connect with other brides and grooms, and to help others by sharing information, your own research, and inspiration.

Websites

Brides and grooms have been using wedding websites for a while now. Many companies offer free wedding websites and some charge a fee; it really depends on the sophistication of the website you want. If you are tech savvy, you can even create and host your own. Websites are different from blogs because although you can update them, they are more static, meaning particular information remains constant. Couples use websites for detailed, pertinent information regarding accommodations, directions/maps, and gift registry links. Some may even take RSVPs through their sites.

No matter which medium you choose, be sure to check the privacy settings on all of your accounts regularly. Even if they are set to private or "friends only," sometimes system upgrades on social media sites reset your personal settings.

How Social Media Can Help

Social media can facilitate your wedding planning. On your lunch hour you can scan Pinterest for great ideas, send off a few e-mails to vendors, and maybe even tweet a couple of companies with questions. The ease and reach of social media is vast and can certainly make life easy, as well as cut down on hours spent doing research.

Before you decide for or against using social media to help you plan your wedding, you must take a look at what it can do for you. When utilized correctly, social media is a great tool, but when not used correctly—when used without a "social filter"—social media can be hurtful and overwhelming, too. Here are some of the ways it can help you:

- ◆ You can connect with wedding suppliers and wedding vendors via social media. "Liking" a company's Facebook page or following a Twitter feed or a blog may give you access to additional discounts, daily deals, insights as to how the vendors work, and almost instant access to them, as well as a glimpse into what others are saying about them online.
- ◆ You can pass along information quickly and easily. This applies not only to your vendors and suppliers but to your invited guests and wedding party as well. Just think about how many people you know who are alerted every time they

receive a text, e-mail, or message/posting on social media. It's instant access!

♦ You can create a group for invited guests (or the wedding party, etc.) on Facebook. If you are going to use groups to disseminate information through social media, you need to make sure the group is private so that not everyone can access it. You cannot assume that everyone wants to hear about the wedding, especially if they are not invited. You can also set up a private blog to share information.

♦ There is no shortage of amazing inspiration for wedding themes, gowns, and décor on the web. Sites such as Pinterest allow you to have your own virtual bulletin board where you can gather ideas and save them for future reference.

♦ You can help faraway family members feel as if they are a part of the planning. Maybe your mom lives out of town; maybe your sister has always imagined being by your side but she just can't be there. Share details about your planning by using Instagram or a smaller private group page on Facebook. You can snap and share photos, upload images, and share all the other details as you plan to help make distant relatives feel that they are included.

How Social Media Can Hurt

For all the good social media can do, it can become too much . . . you can become too much on your social media outlets. Weddings are fun and fabulous and your best friend and mom may want to know every detail, but that does not mean all of your friends and connections do. Brides tend to overshare, and with the ease social media provides, this can become quite the issue. Here are some ways to avoid overusing social media:

- You may want to post your engagement on Facebook. You might want to share all of the details of your event. In fact, a countdown to the big day sounds divine, but hold it right there. Remember that some of your "friends" who are not invited will have hurt feelings. Even though these "friends" may be happy for you, not everyone wants to see and hear about plans for a wedding celebration they won't be a part of. Consider creating a private or smaller group of friends who can see your day-to-day wedding posts.
- Even for those who are invited and a part of the festivities, if you post wedding updates every hour, they are going to get tired of it really quickly. There can be too much of a good thing. If you become obsessed and single-minded with your wedding planning, people are going to tune you out.
- Being obsessed with anything is not pretty. Brides tend to be an obsessive group anyway, and with social media a bride can take it to new levels. Spending your days with your eyes glued to a screen, scrolling through wedding ideas, tweeting vendors, liking Facebook pages, and uploading photos to Instagram can lead to burnout.
- Share too much of your wedding plans and you may end up with unsolicited advice.
- Showing too much before the big day leads you to miss that wow factor with your guests on the wedding day.

Be careful what you say and post on social media. It can be shared and manipulated by hackers, thieves, frenemies, and unseemly characters. And above all—don't post anything online you wouldn't want your mom to know!

Sharing the Big News

A ring. A magical question. A need to tell everyone! Easy, right? Just grab your mobile device, snap a photo, and let the world know you are engaged . . . right? WRONG! It may be tempting to announce the news to almost everyone with a few clicks, but that is not the right way to do it. Read on to find out how to gracefully use social media to plan and communicate.

The Right Way

You may be one half of a modern tweeting, texting, sharing couple, but that does not mean all of your guests are. Or, even if they are, seeing a status update or getting an e-mail may not be the way they want to hear the news of an engagement. With so many options, how do you make it all work? No matter what the inner social media maven inside you says, you must use the telephone if not a face-to-face meeting to tell those closest to you that you are engaged. Your parents, and your fiancé's parents, especially need to be told before you tell the world. But don't stop there. Be sure to tell other close friends and relatives the news before you post it online.

There is really no official time frame or waiting period before you post any updates on your marital status. Some say two weeks, some say never. Most importantly, you need to make sure that those closest to you have been told in person or via telephone (yup, the old-fashioned way!). After that, whether or not you announce your engagement on social media is up to you, but do it subtly and tastefully. And if you do, be warned that there may be those who, after following the news of your planning, will be hurt when they never receive an invitation.

The subtlest way to announce your engagement on Facebook or any other social media site with marital status as an option is to simply change that status on your profile page to Engaged. It is simple, "quiet," and won't leave anyone thinking you are just showing off.

Before you post a picture of your ring on Facebook or elsewhere, make sure that all those important people in your life know the news first. Posting a photo of your ring will be seen by some as sharing a moment of pure bliss and excitement, and by others as showing off, so think about how you want to do this. Perhaps a single shot of the two of you with the ring showing is a better idea than creating an album with seventy-five different angles of the diamond.

Twitter

On Twitter, you can create a list that includes all of those invited to the wedding, but realize your Twitter feed is still public. If you feel the need to tweet, consider setting up a wedding Twitter account with protected tweets, meaning those friends and family members who know about it need to be approved (by you) to follow you.

Facebook

Consider setting up a private group on Facebook. You can create a private page and invite only those who are invited to the wedding. Then you have a private forum to share away and post wedding updates. Anyone who accepts the invitation for the page should be fully aware of what it is for. You can also create multiple groups to accommodate different needs—for example, one for the wedding party and one for your mother, sister, and maid of honor. Just be sure not to make a lot of announcements on your public page telling everyone to "head over to the (private) wedding page to see the latest news." That kind of defeats the purpose.

Instagram

One easy way to keep things private on Instagram is to use direct messaging. Everyone always forgets about this great option! You can use this method to get in touch with anyone, from your bridal party or friends to vendors, photographers, entertainers, and other brides who are sharing information. If you find the perfect florist, or simply love another bride's wedding, send a direct message. Chances are you'll get a response quickly, and your big plans won't be splashed across your Instagram feed.

Pinterest

A simple way to keep track of your big plans without sharing with the rest of your Pinterest followers is to create a private pin board. When you're creating a new board, click the "Secret" toggle to make it private. Only you and anyone you invite can see your secret pins, and they won't appear in the home feed, search fields, or anywhere else on Pinterest. If later you decide you want to share your board publicly, just change the settings on the board's edit page.

The Wrong Way

Be careful not to breach offline etiquette when using online media. For example, posting a gift-giving link on any social media site might seem a little greedy. Such links are best left to the wedding website, where people expect to find them. If someone asks you where to find these links (even if it is in a public forum, such as on your Facebook wall), send him or her a private message with the information.

Keep any negativity associated with your wedding planning offline. Dealing with logistics and money and family can take its toll, but don't air frustrations and dirty laundry online. Too much wedding chatter anywhere, even in real life, will turn people off. That does not mean they are not happy for you, but the rest of the world is simply living everyday life, and probably does not want to be inundated with wedding chatter all day long. Keep control and try to post updates on your private wedding group pages. Also, space your posts out, and don't forget to add in some other nonwedding updates too. Be sure to interact with people on other topics besides your wedding. Remember, you were a person with other interests before you got the ring!

Guest Considerations

There are a lot of ways to make social media work in your wedding plans, but remember that not all guests are social media pros. Grandma may not be into checking a blog or Facebook. For that matter, your parents may not choose to access these tools either. You need to find ways to use social media, but not exclude those who do not use it.

Invitations

Even for the most casual weddings, e-mailing an invitation is not traditionally considered proper. For a formal wedding this would confuse the guests, as the invitation should match the tone and style of the event. But even for a casual affair, an e-mail is too impersonal and too informal a way to invite the people you are closest with to your wedding.

However, some brides are very eco-conscious, and want to save paper. If that's your aim, *how* you use social media is what determines if it is tacky or not. Blasts of information such as, "Engagement party is in two days. Don't forget we are registered at . . ." is tacky. Anything that announces major invite-only events to masses of people who are not invited or is a post disguised as a "don't forget to bring a gift" statement is in bad taste. Using social media to privately communicate with only those who are invited is perfectly acceptable. Private groups and e-mailed updates in conjunction with your blog or website is how information can and should be conveyed. Keep in mind that you'll probably still need offline invitations for some guests.

Live-Streaming the Events

Some guests may be unable to travel to your wedding for health or myriad other reasons, but they can still get a peek at your nuptials! Once upon a time, you would send DVDs or photos to guests who could not attend your wedding. Now, a live-streaming feed of your wedding is the way to share with those who cannot attend. You can DIY (with your Internet connection, a service, and a camera) or you can hire a company that can come in with a professional videographer and set it all up.

Potential Social Media Pitfalls

Unless you are the royal couple and can require that everyone turn off their phones as they arrive at the wedding, you are going to need to contend with social media before or at your wedding. There is a time and place for it, if you want it there. Even if you plan to have an unplugged wedding, someone is going to take a photo and share it online. Someone will tweet. Here are some ways to manage the onslaught.

Handling Negative Interactions

If you choose to put yourself out there by encouraging social media interaction, sadly there may be a person out there somewhere—perhaps one you do not even know—who cannot appreciate the fun of it. Plus, there are always trolls (people looking for trouble) who may make unseemly comments. There are those who, no matter what the situation, cannot say anything nice. There is nothing you can do to stop this.

If you find that a distant "friend" has been saying negative things about you or your wedding on social media, however, your best bet is to contact this friend. Explain the situation and ask her to please stop this behavior. She may think she is being funny . . .

even if neither you nor anyone else is getting the joke. Chances are she just may be immature enough to think that this is a good way to lash out for not being invited. Most social media avenues have ways to block or moderate comments from particular users, which can prevent them from being able to post anything on your feed. If her toxic activity continues, you can also report her to whichever platform she is using for the offensive behavior.

Even if you play nice and use social media appropriately during the planning of your wedding, long-lost friends and family members and even mere acquaintances may be upset if they were not invited. You simply need to explain that your wedding was for those closest to you. If they continue to give you trouble, it may be time to "unfriend" them!

Posting Pictures/Tweeting from the Wedding

With the easy access to phones, computers, tablets, and social media, you must realize you cannot control the flow of everything. If you have taken the steps to invite social media into your wedding day, some guests may have a hard time realizing that there is a line that should not be crossed. Someone may make an insensitive comment or post an unflattering photo—this is simply the reality of the time we live in. Hopefully it won't happen, but you should be prepared.

Most experts agree that texting and tweeting during a ceremony should be off-limits. No guest should stand up mid-ceremony to get a better photo so they can Instagram it. It is just common sense. However, common sense seems to be disappearing quickly. If the guests are involved in social media interactions when they should be attentive and part of the larger event, it is considered rude.

If you'd prefer that your guests *not* post pictures or information directly from your wedding, you can e-mail the most likely suspects (chances are good that you'll know who the potential offenders might be), and politely ask them to refrain. You could tell your friends that you'll post a link to professional photos later, or that you'll post a few selections (that you choose!) when you return from your honeymoon. You can also have the ushers pass out cards to the guests with a few notes, such as: "please refrain from tweeting during the ceremony," and "please do not post wedding photos until the couple has."

Another area of potential concern: many professional photographers post a few client photos on their Facebook page to show their work to others. If you're not comfortable with yours posting photos of you and your partner, speak with your photographer. Ultimately, he or she should not post anything until you have agreed to it and given your approval. Just explain your concerns, and add a clause to the contract.

Finally, you may find companies contacting you to provide you with supplies or their product in exchange for links, a mention in your wedding program, etc. Do not be lured in by the idea of free stuff. "Sponsored weddings" are the tackiest of all.

Planning an Unplugged Wedding

On this most important day, it is understandable that you want your closest friends and family to be fully present with you, rather than distracted by tweets, photos, or Facebook posts. For this reason, many couples are asking their guests to shut down their mobile devices during their weddings. If you'd like your wedding to be unplugged, consider making a sign to greet guests as they enter the ceremony location or reception site. You could also place a note on the wedding program. Keep your message brief—express your gratitude for their presence at your wedding, and politely encourage them to respect your wishes. (It helps to assure guests that you will share your beautiful photos with them after the day is over!)

The Unplugged Ceremony

If an entire day without social media seems impossible to you, but you still wish to keep social media out of your ceremony, consider asking guests to unplug during the ceremony only. Again, inviting guests to be fully present with you during the ceremony will drive home the point that your wedding should be an event shared with those you love most—and emphasize the fact that photography during the ceremony should be left to the professionals you hired. After the ceremony, guests can feel free to snap photos and share the wedding joy with the rest of the world.

Preventing Photography Mishaps

While many couples encourage guests to snap as many photos as possible, others are asking guests to shut their phones, cameras, and other devices off for the day. Guests snapping photos during the ceremony is particularly distracting, for you as the bride and groom, for officiants, and for other guests. No one appreciates distant relatives sneaking up to the altar to snap photos and live-tweet during the vows. And though they mean well, guests standing in the aisles to get a clearer shot can end up showing up in your formal photos, taking away from the ceremony and the focus on you. (Some guests have even been so brazen as to run up to couples to snap photos during the first dance!)

Flash from other cameras can disrupt (or completely ruin!) shots being taken by the professional photographers you've hired. It's heartbreaking to see completely whitewashed images of you and your spouse, or red or green dots on your white dress from focusing beams. Having an unplugged wedding is a great way to discourage these things from happening, and while it can't guarantee your guests will abide by the rules, it will make them more aware of their actions during your big day.

Encouraging Social Media Use at the Wedding

On the other hand entirely, maybe you want to harness social media at your wedding and use it to its full capacity! Maybe you and your partner think it will be cool to see photos and posts about your wedding on various social media outlets. If so, here are some ways to do that.

Create a Hashtag

If you want guests to share as much as possible from your wedding, you should create a wedding hashtag—a phrase that guests can use on Twitter and Instagram to gather and share photos from the day. You can create something as simple as your last names or wedding date (such as #SmithWestWedding or #JamieandJacob2017), or get creative to set your wedding apart from the pack. Try fun, celebrified names like #Bennifer or #Amanthony; rhymes like #WeSaidIDoOnMay22; or whimsical or funny names, like #JessandJuneinWonderland, #TheBestWeddingEver, or #WedLongAndProsper.

Post signs at your ceremony or reception site with your hashtag name and ask folks to tweet and Instagram their pics with it. That way, when the big day is over, you'll be able to search photos by the hashtag and enjoy seeing photos from your guests' perspectives!

Name Someone a "Social Media Manager"

Surely you have a tech-savvy friend—a social media master of sorts. Ask this person if he or she would help you out on your wedding day. He or she would be in charge of making sure the guests know what your wedding's hashtag is on Twitter, relaying user and group names for other social media outlets, and compiling the posted information after the wedding. Perhaps this person would be responsible for creating a display of the photos and tweets that happened during the wedding and presenting them at the reception.

Consider Having a "Head Tweeter"

Some couples dream of having their wedding trend on Twitter. Since you and your partner will be busy on the wedding day (and probably not tweeting much yourself), how can you do this? You need a head tweeter or a Tweeter of Honor (or whatever name you want to call it). You may even want more than one!

Head tweeters can ask or remind their followers to pass the word around and use the wedding hashtag. They may even tweet celebrities asking them to send out the tweet as well (no guarantees!). This can ultimately be their job on the wedding day. If you are truly making this a social media event, ask the tweeters to visit guests and ask them to tweet or even ask for the words and tweet for them. If you really want to take it over the top, have one of the tweeters read some of the well wishes (at some point) during the reception.

CHAPTER 6

Showers and Other Parties

ONE GREAT PERK of following the traditional road to your wedding day is that you'll suddenly find yourself in the middle of a gift-giving storm. Although you won't be hosting a party for yourself, whoever hosts your shower (or engagement party, for that matter) will probably be looking for your opinion on any number of issues, such as the guest list, the menu, and games.

The Engagement Party

Although it is customary for the family of the bride to host some sort of an engagement party, it's perfectly acceptable for the family of the groom (or anyone else) to host such an affair—or for you to do without one altogether, if you prefer. Most engagement parties nowadays are very informal, with invites being done via phone calls or electronic invitations. The party is usually held either at the host's home or in a restaurant. Guests do not typically bring gifts to an engagement party.

The Bridal Shower

This is the big prewedding party. In the past, etiquette dictated that a bridal shower could only be hosted by your friends, not by family. Today, as with almost all things wedding-related, etiquette has changed. Family, friends, coworkers, or anyone else who is so inclined can throw a shower for you. Usually your attendants, in combination with your mother and other close family members, will pony up and play hostesses—but who knows what other generous people might have a party up their sleeve?

Where and When

Typically, a shower is held either at a small function hall or in someone's home, depending on the size of the guest list. In the past, this was an event strictly for women, but it's becoming more and more common for the fiancé to join the festivities. He probably won't be nearly as excited as you are about the pots and pans, measuring spoons, and placemats—but you never know. "Jack and Jill" showers—where attendants from both sides host and attend—are also becoming more common.

In the past, the specifics of the shower (time, date, location, and so on) were kept secret from the bride until the last possible moment. These days, however, it's common, and in many cases necessary, for the bride to take an active part in planning the festivities.

Showers are usually held two to three months before the wedding date. If you absolutely cannot corral your most important guests within the confines of this period, shoot for a slightly earlier date (say, three and a half months before the ceremony)—or one that's a little closer to the wedding (but no less than a month before the big day). A date that's too close, however, might set you up for feeling stressed over last-minute wedding details while trying to squeeze your shower in somewhere.

The Guest List

Making up a guest list? Check with your host(s) first and touch base on the budget. If the plan is for your shower to be a small, informal affair in someone's tiny apartment, obviously your list will be much different than if it's going to be in a huge banquet hall. In either case, who should be invited, and who should be left off the list? The cardinal rule is that any guest who is invited to the shower is automatically invited to the wedding. Make sure that your hosts are only inviting preapproved wedding guests.

Shower Size

No matter how small the shower, the guests should be treated to a nice little party. They should be fed, champagned, and entertained. You might cringe at the idea of shower games, and if you're inviting a small group of women who feel the same way, you can encourage your hosts to do away with the games and the door prizes altogether. Just be aware that if your guest list includes women from older generations, those games and prizes are part and parcel of a wedding shower as far as they're concerned.

The bride with a large family and many close friends often finds herself in the midst of a large shower. Some brides feel overwhelmed by the attention and the sheer volume of gifts generated by a party of this magnitude. Here are a few tips for navigating the large shower:

* **Keep cool.** Even if you're completely overwhelmed, every guest wants to see you looking happy.
* **Mingle.** All of these women have come to celebrate your impending marriage, and they brought you gifts. Say hello to every single one of them.
* **Feed yourself.** You're going to have a long afternoon. If you know that you become easily irritated when you feel crowded or hungry, don't turn a potentially bad situation into a disaster by not eating.
* **Fudge it.** Every gift deserves a sincere (or at least sincere-sounding) ooh and/or ahh, even if you find you're losing steam when you're only halfway through the pile.

Keeping Track of Gifts

During the gift-opening part of the shower, put someone you trust (an organized bridesmaid, your mother, a friend—not your six-year-old niece) in charge of recording each gift and who gave it. Make sure the person charged with keeping track of the gifts understands the importance of the task. Choose someone who can stay focused even if things get hectic, so when you write your thank-you notes, you won't come off sounding like a confused bride. You don't want to thank your Aunt Marion for the gift that Aunt Mary gave you, or vice versa.

Truly Personal Invitations

These days, software and online invitation sites have taken the financial bite out of ordering unique invitations. But brides and/or their

BRIDAL SHOWER GUEST LIST WORKSHEET

Name: ....

Address: ....

....

Telephone: ....

○ RSVP   Number in Party: ____
....

Name: ....

Address: ....

....

Telephone: ....

○ RSVP   Number in Party: ____
....

Name: ....

Address: ....

....

Telephone: ....

○ RSVP   Number in Party: ____
....

Name: ....

Address: ....

....

Telephone: ....

○ RSVP   Number in Party: ____
....

Name: ....

Address: ....

....

Telephone: ....

○ RSVP   Number in Party: ____
....

Name: ....

Address: ....

....

Telephone: ....

○ RSVP   Number in Party: ____
....

Name: ....

Address: ....

....

Telephone: ....

○ RSVP   Number in Party: ____
....

Name: ....

Address: ....

....

Telephone: ....

○ RSVP   Number in Party: ____
....

Name: ....

Address: ....

....

Telephone: ....

○ RSVP   Number in Party: ____

....

Name: ....

Address: ....

....

Telephone: ....

○ RSVP   Number in Party: ____

....

Name: ....

Address: ....

....

Telephone: ....

○ RSVP   Number in Party: ____

....

Name: ....

Address: ....

....

Telephone: ....

○ RSVP   Number in Party: ____

....

Name: ....

Address: ....

....

Telephone: ....

○ RSVP   Number in Party: ____

....

Name: ....

Address: ....

....

Telephone: ....

○ RSVP   Number in Party: ____

....

Name: ....

Address: ....

....

Telephone: ....

○ RSVP   Number in Party: ____

....

Name: ....

Address: ....

....

Telephone: ....

○ RSVP   Number in Party: ____

....

attendants or family members who have a crafty streak sometimes like to make their own invites—something they can literally put their own mark on. Here's one idea for creating your own shower invitation—keep in mind, you can change the colors, the design, or the wording to suit your own style.

For twenty-five invitations, you'll need:

◆ Printed piece: (25) 4¼" × 5½" card stock (A2 size), white or off-white
◆ Base: (25) 4⅝" × 6¼" card size (A6 size), color determined by your wedding
◆ Envelope: (25) 4⅝" × 6¼" card size (A6 size), color determined by your wedding
◆ Spool of ¼" ribbon, same color as the larger card stock
◆ 10 sheets vellum
◆ Tape gun
◆ Hole puncher

Before you begin assembly of the invitation, print the information for the shower on the smaller card stock using your computer.

1. Take a sheet of the vellum and cut a 2"-wide strip, lengthwise.
2. Use the tape gun to run adhesive along the back of the strip.
3. Place the vellum strip, adhesive side down, in the center of the base, also lengthwise. Press firmly. The vellum strip will be longer than the base card—simply take the ends, fold them over to the other side, and press firmly.
4. Now, take the printed card stock. Run adhesive along the back. Center the printed card stock on the base card and press firmly.
5. Using a pencil, make a small mark at the top center of the printed piece. Punch two holes about ½" on either side of the mark.

6. Cut a length of ribbon, about 4" long. Flip the card over and thread the ends through both holes.
7. Flip the card back to the front. Tie the ribbon.
8. Slip the invitation into one of your waiting envelopes.

Coil Up a Fun Centerpiece

If you've been to a number of bridal showers, you've no doubt seen your fair share of floral centerpieces, which are lovely—but costly. If you're looking to keep costs down and have a little fun with your centerpieces, try this Towel Cake centerpiece. It's cute, it's different, and it's useful!

You will need:

- 2 bath towels
- 2 hand towels
- 2 washcloths
- Assorted safety pins
- Faux rings from a craft store
- Silk flowers—large and small roses work well
- Decorations to suit your style—faux pearls, beads, etc.
- Cake plate
- Ribbon (the color of your bridesmaids' dresses, or a close approximation)

1. Take the first bath towel, and fold it in thirds lengthwise. Now fold the resulting skinny towel in half. Do the same to the second bath towel.
2. Tack the two (folded) bath towels together with safety pins.
3. Start at one end of the now-joined bath towels and coil tightly. This will be the large base of the cake.

4. When the base is coiled, wrap with ribbon to hold it firmly together. Close the ribbon with a small safety pin. You'll be able to hide the pin under the silk flowers and other "cake" decorations (which can also be pinned on with small safety pins).
5. Now, do the same with the hand towels. Fold, tack together, and coil. Wrap with ribbon; close ribbon with safety pin.
6. Follow the same instructions with the washcloths.
7. Stack the layers of towels to resemble a wedding cake and attach with large safety pins.

You've just made a fun centerpiece, suitable for a gift or buffet table, and it can double as a door prize. (Who doesn't need a few extra towels?)

The Bachelor Party

In the past, this party was held the night before the wedding, but too many hungover grooms and weaving, green groomsmen have led more and more rational adults to the conclusion that the bachelor party is better suited for an earlier date. If you can convince your groom to have this party at least two weeks before the wedding, everyone will feel better about the whole thing. A week before the big day is the closest he should try to squeeze it in.

The Bachelorette Party

Bachelorettes have come a long way in the past decade, so most brides fully expect to paint the town red with their best gal pals. Your friends may spend months planning the perfect bachelorette party for you, complete with male strippers, great food, awesome music, a limo . . . and whatever else they can cook up. The same time frame applies as for the bachelor party. You don't want to try to juggle a hangover and your wedding day.

Bridesmaids' Luncheon/Attendants' Party

An attendants' party gives you the chance to turn the tables—to honor the people who've been honoring (and assisting) you. Usually this party is scheduled a week or two before the wedding, to give all the harried planners a chance to relax. And it gives you a chance to thank them for all that they have done for you during this busy time.

This may be the perfect time to give your attendants the gifts you've bought for them (though if you want to wait until the rehearsal dinner, that's fine, too). The guest list does not have to be limited to the attendants; family and close friends can also be included. To keep the atmosphere relaxed, consider having a barbecue, a park picnic, or a day at the beach. You might also want to consider taking a hiatus from wedding talk. Make it a day (or night) to concentrate on what's going on in your attendants' lives. You may have been missing out on some good stuff while you were caught up in your own wedding whirlwind.

BRIDAL SHOWER GIFT RECORDER WORKSHEET

Name	Description of Gift	Thank-You Note Sent?

BACHELORETTE PARTY GUEST LIST WORKSHEET

Name: ....
Address: ....
....
Telephone: ....
○ RSVP   Number in Party: ____
....

Name: ....
Address: ....
....
Telephone: ....
○ RSVP   Number in Party: ____
....

Name: ....
Address: ....
....
Telephone: ....
○ RSVP   Number in Party: ____
....

Name: ....
Address: ....
....
Telephone: ....
○ RSVP   Number in Party: ____
....

Name: ....
Address: ....
....
Telephone: ....
○ RSVP   Number in Party: ____
....

Name: ....
Address: ....
....
Telephone: ....
○ RSVP   Number in Party: ____
....

Name: ....
Address: ....
....
Telephone: ....
○ RSVP   Number in Party: ____
....

Name: ....
Address: ....
....
Telephone: ....
○ RSVP   Number in Party: ____
....

ATTENDANTS' PARTY WORKSHEET

Location:
....

Telephone:
....

Contact:
....

Date:
....

Time:
....

Directions:
....

....

Number of guests:
....

Menu:
....

....

Beverages:
....

....

Activities:
....

....

Other:
....

....

....

Cost:
....

Notes:
....

....

....

....

CHAPTER 7

The Ceremony

THE WEDDING CEREMONY: it's that little thing you have to get through before you can get to the reception and your honeymoon. This is where you make the official commitment. You'll enter as an engaged couple and come out married! The ceremony sets the scene for the rest of the day, so you don't want to leave anything to chance. The wedding of your dreams is in the details, after all.

Religious or Civil?

Squaring away the details of your wedding ceremony should be one of your first priorities. If you don't know the location, date, and time of your ceremony, then you can't do much of the reception planning. You'll first need to decide whether you prefer a religious or civil ceremony. If you are interested in having a religious ceremony, consult with your officiant as soon as possible about the availability of the church or synagogue for the date you've selected. You will also want to know of any restrictions and guidelines that will apply.

An alternative for those who are unsure of their religious convictions but want to incorporate spirituality into their wedding ceremony is the nondenominational wedding ceremony. This is a spiritual ceremony without the structure and restrictions of one specific religion, although the service typically resembles a traditional Protestant ceremony. This type of ceremony is offered by the Unitarian Universalist church and other nondenominational groups that perform interfaith marriages for nonmembers.

Let's Be Civil!

Some couples faced with the tension and potential family problems of an interfaith marriage choose a civil ceremony. Other couples choose to go this route because they aren't particularly religious people, because they're looking to avoid the expense of a traditional church wedding, or because they're short on time. Civil ceremonies are usually quite a bit easier to pull together than a ceremony in a church.

Contrary to the assumption (a barren scene in a judge's chambers that takes all of twenty seconds), a civil ceremony does not necessarily mean boring, quick, or small. You can have a civil ceremony with all the trimmings of a traditional wedding. After all, your civic official isn't tied to the chair in city hall. Get him out of the office—and over to a hotel ballroom, a country club, a yacht, or any other place where you feel like having your wedding.

Civil ceremonies not held at city hall or a courthouse are usually held at the reception site, which tends to make things more convenient for all involved. The party simply moves from one area of the ballroom or country club to another after the vows are recited.

Religious Ceremonies

The specifics of religious ceremonies vary from religion to religion and denomination to denomination. Your officiant will be able to explain in more detail what's involved, but following is a quick rundown.

Meeting with the Officiant

If you decide to have a religious ceremony, consult with your officiant about premarital requirements as soon as you can. Religions differ in their rules and restrictions, as do different sects within the same religion. If you're involved in your church (and/or have been to many weddings in it), you probably have some idea of what lies ahead. However, if you don't attend services regularly, or if you're planning to have the ceremony in your fiancé's church, you might not have the faintest idea of what's allowed and what's not.

Your first meeting with the officiant should clear up most of the technical details and give you the opportunity to ask questions. After everything is settled, the way will be clear for you to personalize the ceremony with music, Scripture readings, special prayers, and even your own vows.

During the meeting with your officiant, be sure to get all the details concerning rules and restrictions, the church's stance on interfaith marriages (if applicable), any required commitments to raise children in the religion, and so on. Don't be afraid to ask questions. You want to make sure you and the church are on the same wavelength regarding these important issues:

- What are the requirements (including any premarital counseling) for getting married in this church/synagogue?
- Are interfaith ceremonies permitted? What are the requirements or restrictions involved?
- Is the date (and time) you're interested in available?
- Who will perform the ceremony? (You may be close to a particular officiant, only to find that he is not available at the time you want.)
- Are visiting clergy allowed to take part in the ceremony? If so, who will be responsible for what?
- Are there any restrictions on decorations? On music?
- Is another wedding scheduled for the same day as yours? Is there adequate time between the ceremonies so that your guests and the other guests aren't fighting for parking spots?
- Are there any restrictions on where the photographer and videographer can stand (or move) during the ceremony? Is flash photography allowed?
- Will you be allowed to hold a receiving line on-site (in the back of the church or synagogue, or in a courtyard, for instance)?

You should also ask about the cost for the ceremony and for the use of church or synagogue personnel and facilities. This payment is typically referred to as a donation. It doesn't go to any single individual, but to the church or synagogue as a whole.

Online Ministers

When it comes down to choosing the person who will hear your vows and pronounce you and your beloved married, some

OFFICIANT WORKSHEET

Officiant/Clergy:
....

Address:
....

Telephone:

FIRST MEETING

Date and time:
....

Location:
....

Notes:
....

SECOND MEETING

Date and time:
....

Location:
....

Notes:
....

THIRD MEETING

Date and time:
....

Location:
....

Notes:
....

FOURTH MEETING

Date and time:
....

Location:
....

Notes:
....

FIFTH MEETING

Date and time:
....

Location:
....

Notes:
....

ADDITIONAL MEETINGS

Date and time:
....

Location:
....

Notes:
....

....

Fee:
....

Notes:
....

....

Date and time:
....

Location:
....

Notes:
....

....

Fee:
....

Notes:
....

couples find themselves in a quandary. They want a very personal experience, but if they aren't regular churchgoers and/or don't happen to have a judge, a rabbi, a minister, or a priest in the family, they feel as though they're stuck working with an officiant who may or may not understand their wants and needs.

Some couples turn to friends, asking them to become online ordained ministers. If you think about it, it makes sense: Online ordination is a fairly simple process, in many cases it's free, and it does make for a very personal ceremony. One caveat: check the laws for marriage in your state. If a minister has to be affiliated with a brick-and-mortar church in order to perform marriages, you'll either have to go the more traditional route . . . or move your wedding to a location that's more hospitable to modern ministry!

For more information on online ordination, check out these websites:

- www.themonastery.org
- www.amfellow.org
- www.spiritualhumanism.org

Writing Your Own Vows

Expressing oneself on paper comes easy for some people; for others, it's nothing less than pure torture. And expressing oneself in public causes distress for a whole lot of people. When it comes to reciting your own wedding vows, though, most couples find they are willing to dig deep and make the effort. They picture themselves at the altar, under the chuppah, at the seaside—wherever the wedding is going to take place—staring into each other's eyes, saying . . . what, exactly?

And that's where the problem lies. If you haven't written anything since your senior year in high school, you may not even know where to begin with your wedding vows. There's so much to

CEREMONY PLANNING WORKSHEET

Location of ceremony:
....

Address:
....

....

Date of ceremony:
....

Time of ceremony:
....

Officiant's name:
....

Location fee:
....

Officiant's fee:
....

Recommended church/synagogue donation:
....

Wedding program available?
....

Fee:

Part of Ceremony	Notes
Processional	
Opening words	
Giving away or blessing	
Reading	
Prayers	
Marriage vows	
Exchange of rings	
Pronouncement of marriage	
Lighting of unity candle	
Benediction	
Closing words	
Recessional	
Other	

say—are you expected to cover every aspect of your relationship?! Nah. You'd be there for hours, and you have a reception to get to!

The best way to approach writing your vows is to choose a theme. For example:

- **How you met.** What was special about it? Was it serendipitous, or silly, or did you dislike each other at your first meeting? If you had not met at all, where would you be now?
- **How your relationship has transformed your life.** Maybe your partner saved you from life in the fast lane; or maybe he brought you out of your shell. How would your life have been different if you had not met this person?
- **Your love.** How do you feel when you think about your fiancé, and when you imagine life fifty years from now with him? How do you envision your love growing and changing?

Of course, you can combine these in any way, or go in another direction altogether. The point is not to ramble. Know what you want to say and stay on point. Your vows will be meaningful to you and your fiancé, and your guests will be scrambling for their tissues.

Levels of Formality

The time and location of the wedding ceremony, the type of reception, and the attire of the wedding party and guests are just a few elements that contribute to the level of your wedding's formality. Listed below are some general guidelines to follow regarding your type of wedding. Choose whatever feels right to you and your fiancé. Just remember, whatever level of formality you choose, try to keep it more or less consistent in every aspect throughout.

PERSONALIZING YOUR VOWS WORKSHEET

Answer together: How do you, as a couple, define the following terms?

Love:

....

....

....

Trust:

....

....

....

Marriage:

....

....

....

Family:

....

....

....

Commitment:

....

....

....

Togetherness:

....

....

....

Answer together: How did the two of you first meet?

....

....

....

Answer separately: What was the first thing you noticed about your partner?

Bride:

....

....

Groom:

....

....

Answer together: List any shared hobbies or mutual interests you share.

....

....

....

Answer together: What was the single most important event in your relationship? (Or what is the event that you feel says the most about your development as a couple?)

....

....

....

Answer together: How similar (or different) were your respective childhoods? Take a moment and try to recount some of the important parallels here.

....

....

....

Answer together: Is there a song, poem, or book that is particularly meaningful in your relationship? If so, identify it here.

....

....

....

Answer together: Do you and your partner share a common religious tradition? If so, identify it here.

....

....

....

Answer together: Why did your parents' marriages succeed or fail? What marital pitfalls do you want to avoid? What can you take from your parents' examples, good or bad?

....

....

....

....

Answer together: Take some time to reminisce about the course of your relationship. When did you first realize you loved each other? When did you first say the words? What trials and tribulations has your love had to overcome? What shared memories are you most fond of?

....

....

....

Answer separately: What do you love about your partner? Why?

Bride:

....

....

Groom:

....

....

Answer together: How do you and your partner look at personal growth and change? What aspects of your life together are likely to change over the coming years? How do you anticipate dealing with those changes? How important is mutual respect and tolerance in your relationship? When one of you feels that a particular need is being overlooked, what do you feel is the best way to address this problem with the other person?

....

....

....

....

Answer together: Do you and your partner have a common vision of what your life will be like as older people? Will it include children or grandchildren? Take this opportunity to put into words the vision you and your partner share of what it will be like to grow old together.

....

....

....

....

....

Very Formal

- Formal ceremony in a church, synagogue, or luxury hotel
- 200 or more guests
- Engraved invitations with traditional typeface and wording
- Four to six attendants each for the bride and the groom
- Veil, gloves, and gown with a cathedral-length train for the bride
- Floor-length dresses or gowns for the bridesmaids
- Formal attire (white tie and coattails for evening) for the groom, groomsmen, and guests
- Elaborate sit-down dinner, usually held in a ballroom
- Live band or orchestra
- Elaborate cascade bouquets and floral displays
- Antique cars or limousines

Formal

- Formal ceremony in a church, synagogue, or luxury hotel
- 100 or more guests
- Engraved or printed invitations with traditional wording
- Three to six attendants each for the bride and the groom
- Elegant gown with a chapel-length or sweeping train and veil for the bride
- Floor-length dresses or gowns for the bridesmaids
- Formal attire (black tie for evening) for the groom, grooms-men, and guests
- Sit-down dinner or buffet in a ballroom, banquet facility, or private club
- Live band or disc jockey
- Medium-sized bouquets and floral displays
- Horse-drawn carriages, antique cars, or limousines

Semiformal

- Semiformal ceremony in a church, synagogue, private home, outdoors, or other location
- Fewer than 100 guests
- Printed invitations with traditional or personalized wording
- One to three attendants each for the bride and the groom
- Floor- or cocktail-length gown with a fingertip veil or hat for the bride
- Floor- or cocktail-length dresses for the bridesmaids
- Nice suits and ties for groom, groomsmen, and male guests
- Semiformal reception including a simple meal or light refreshments at ceremony location
- Live band or disc jockey
- Small bouquet for the bride, simple flower arrangements for decorations
- Town car or limousine

Informal

- Daytime ceremony often held at home or in a judge's chambers
- Fewer than 50 guests
- Printed or handwritten invitations with personalized wording
- One attendant each for the bride and the groom
- Cocktail-length dress or suit, with no veil or train for bride
- Street-length dress for maid or matron of honor
- Nice suits and ties for groom and best man
- Relaxed reception including a simple meal or light refreshments at a home or a restaurant
- Small bouquet or corsage for the bride, simple flower arrangements for decorations

CHAPTER 8

Style for the Aisle

BELIEVE IT OR NOT, some brides hate to shop and the question of what type of dress to wear is more of a stressor than anything. Should it be formal, informal, white, off-white? Should your fiancé wear a white tie, black tie, or no tie? Relax. Now that you know what kind of wedding you're planning, you can move on and find a great wedding style for yourself and your attendants.

The Dress!

Before you leap into the challenging task of finding a wedding gown, do a little homework. First, think about your price range and the general dress style you're looking for.

Style Guidelines

Brides are supposed to follow the informal/formal and time-of-day guidelines based on the type of wedding they're planning. However, many brides are choosing the gowns that they want and happily disregarding these guidelines.

When buying a gown, your major considerations will be the following:

* **Fabric.** While many fabrics do double duty as warm- and cold-weather coverings these days, you should save heavy fabrics, such as silk brocade, for winter weddings. Choose the very light fabrics, such as chiffon, for spring and summer.
* **Sleeves.** Can you wear a sleeveless gown in the coldest months? Yes. Just bring along a formal wrap in case you get chilly. Likewise, if you want to wear long sleeves in July, be prepared to be a bit warm!
* **Length.** If you're having an informal ceremony, a lacy or light-colored dress or suit is fine. If you're having a very formal wedding, choose a floor-length dress with a very long train. For a semiformal wedding, either a tea-length (a length that hits about the mid-calf region) or floor-length gown is a good choice.

Trains

When talking about trains, there are two things you'll want to keep in mind: length and style. Although there are other options, the three most common lengths are sweep, chapel, and cathedral. You can also find shorter trains that fall to your fingertips.

- ◆ **Sweep train:** just touches (or sweeps, get it?) the floor
- ◆ **Chapel train:** trails three to four feet behind the gown
- ◆ **Cathedral (or Monarch) train:** trails six to eight feet behind the gown
- ◆ **Royal Cathedral train:** extends ten (or more) feet behind the gown
- ◆ **Watteau train:** falls from the shoulder blades to the hem of the gown

Bride's Attendants' Attire

At this point, all members of the bridal party should have a good idea of what they're supposed to be doing and when they're supposed to do it. All that's left to decide is what they're going to be wearing while they do it.

Color Your Wedding

First, decide on your wedding colors. These should be colors you *really* like, because you'll be seeing them on your bridesmaids, your flowers, your wedding favors, your decorations, and even your cake. If you have a couple of favorites that go well together, choose both of them. Having trouble deciding? There are some guidelines that can help. If your wedding will be in one of the warmer months, cool pastel shades like ice blue and pale pink work very well. In cooler months, forest green, midnight blue, burgundy, or other warm tones can give the wedding a cozy feel.

The Search

Start looking for your attendants' dresses as soon as you finalize the wedding party. The women need to begin the attire process early because their dresses have to be ordered (or made) and altered.

BRIDE'S ATTIRE WORKSHEET

BRIDAL SALON

Name of salon:
....

Address:
....

Telephone:
....

Salesperson: Store hours:
....

Directions:
....

....

Notes:
....

....

WEDDING GOWN

Description:
....

....

Manufacturer:
....

Style number: Color:
....

Cost: Order date:
....

Deposit paid: Date:
....

Balance due: Date:
....

Fitting date:
....

Delivery date and time:
....

Delivery instructions/Pick-up date:
....

Terms of cancellation:
....

Notes:
....

....

BRIDE'S ATTIRE WORKSHEET (CONTINUED)

HEADPIECE AND VEIL

Description:
....

....

Manufacturer:
....

Style number: Color:
....

Cost: Order date:
....

Deposit paid: Date:
....

Balance due: Date:
....

Delivery date and time:
....

Delivery instructions/Pick-up date:
....

....

Notes:
....

....

Bridal Accessory	Description	Cost	Where Purchased (if different from above)	Picked Up?
Slip:				
Bra:				
Hosiery:				
Garter:				
Gloves:				
Shoes:				
Jewelry:				
Other:				

When searching for your attendants' gowns, check the formal dress section of a quality department store in your area before you go to a bridal salon. You may find appropriate dresses they can wear again in the future—and at a lower price than salon dresses.

Attendants do not have to troop to the bridal salon as a group for fittings. Once they have ordered their dresses, they can go for alterations at their own convenience; just be sure to give them a deadline for getting it all done. If one of your bridesmaids lives far away and can't make it to town for the fittings, ask your salon about alternate arrangements. If you can, e-mail or text her a photo of the dress you have in mind, and make sure it's something she will feel comfortable wearing. Then ask her for her measurements so that you can order her dress along with the others. Once the dress comes in, send it to her so she can have alterations done at a tailor where she lives.

Reasonable Options

Around the world, bridesmaids have two common complaints:

1. "The dress I have to wear is hideous."
2. "That hideous dress that I have to wear cost me [insert outrageous price here]."

Luckily, there is a way around the torture of the attendants. Many brides these days are choosing the designer, the color, or the style of dress and then allowing their bridesmaids to finalize the decision. For example, you may see an off-the-shoulder design that would fit and flatter every one of your girls. If it comes in five different hues, let them choose the color that suits each one best. Or you may simply say, "Buy a black, sleeveless, knee-length, classy dress and meet me at the church on time."

If this trend is easiest for you and your attendants, go for it. You'll find that they will be incredibly grateful, and will be more at ease during the ceremony and reception than if they were wearing ill-fitting or cumbersome getups.

The Other Women

A junior bridesmaid can wear the same dress as the other bridesmaids, or you might choose a different style for her that is more appropriate for her age. In a black-and-white wedding, she should not wear solid black; a solid white dress (or one with a black pattern or trimming) is more appropriate.

Flower girls wear either long or short dresses that match or complement the other dresses. If you have a hard time finding something appropriate, don't fret. A white dress trimmed with lace or fabric that matches the other dresses is a lovely option for flower girls.

The mother of the bride usually has first choice when it comes to picking out a style and color for her gown. She then consults with the mother of the groom, who (you hope) picks out a dress color and style that complements, rather than copies, the bride's mother's dress.

Frugal Brides, Unite!

There is nothing more exciting than your first foray into the bridal shop world. The dresses! The personal service! The champagne! The price tags!

And that's where the excitement ends for many women, who find themselves wondering aloud, "Who would pay $5,000 for a dress you can only wear once?!"

Lest you feel slightly ashamed for thinking this way, be assured that this is a very reasonable—and rational—response. And fortunately, there are plenty of ways to keep your costs down in this area:

BRIDE'S ATTENDANTS' ATTIRE WORKSHEET

PLACE OF PURCHASE

Name:
....

Address:
....

....

Telephone:
....

Salesperson: .... Store hours: ....

Directions:
....

....

Notes:
....

....

ATTENDANTS' ATTIRE

Description of dress:
....

....

Manufacturer:
....

Style number: .... Color: ....

Cost per dress: .... Number ordered: ....

Total cost of dresses: .... Order date: ....

Sizes ordered:
....

Deposit paid: .... Date: ....

Balance due: .... Date: ....

Fitting date:
....

Delivery date and time:
....

Delivery instructions/Pick-up date:
....

....

Description of alterations:
....

Alterations fee (total):

....

Description of accessories (hosiery, shoes, jewelry, etc.):

....

....

....

....

Cost of accessories:

....

Cost of dying shoes
  (if applicable):   Color:

....

Notes:

....

....

....

....

MAID/MATRON OF HONOR

Name:

....

Dress size: Shoe size:

....

Other sizes:

....

Fitting date #1:   Time:

....

Fitting date #2:   Time:

....

Fitting date #3:   Time:

....

Notes:

....

....

....

....

- **Look at white or off-white bridesmaid dresses.** Many are beautifully designed and can be yours for several hundred dollars, instead of several thousand.
- **Visit consignment shops.** Not all consignment stores carry bridal gowns, but many do. Even if you have to have a secondhand dress altered to fit, it will still cost less than buying one brand-new.
- **Go online.** Check out eBay or the classified section of your local newspaper online for never-worn or secondhand dresses. You have more leeway to haggle here, and again, the dress plus the price of alterations will come to much less than what you'd spend on a new dress.
- **Borrow.** Have a sister, cousin, friend, or another relative who has recently walked down the aisle? She may be willing to lend you her dress, as long as you offer to have it cleaned after the ceremony.
- **Go nontraditional.** Sure, bridal dresses in this country are usually white and formal, but there's no rule on the books that says you have to wear such an outfit. Branch out. Choose a dress or suit that you love and will wear again.

No matter what you choose to wear, make sure that you are comfortable with your decision. It doesn't matter what your Aunt Peg or Grandma Lu are going to think. You are a grown woman making your own choices. Now go find that inexpensive dress!

Sew You Think You Can Make a Dress . . .

Designer-types and crafty brides-to-be want, more than anything, a dress that will reflect their very individual styles. If you have the time and the wherewithal, there's no reason you shouldn't make your own dress—it's the ultimate personal statement on your wedding day, and you can be sure that your guests will *ooh* and *ahh* over your unique creation. If you're feeling up to the challenge, give yourself plenty of time, and be sure it's within your talent level. You'll need to find a pattern, modify it if necessary, create a mockup dress (using less expensive fabric!), *then* begin sewing and fitting your actual dress.

Accessories

You've found (or made) the perfect dress, but you still need a veil, a headpiece, and all of the little things to complete your ensemble. Although bridal salons offer slips, nylons, bras, and shoes, the items they sell are often overpriced. You're better off buying them elsewhere. The key is starting early enough so that you can find what you need without being pressured for time. Items to add to your list:

- **The veil.** Your headpiece and veil should complement the style of your dress. Don't pick something so elaborate that it overpowers you and your dress.
- **A handbag.** Think little, white, lacy, beaded, or bowed. (Some dressmakers will make drawstring bridal bags from fabric that matches or complements your dress.)
- **Footwear.** Gone are the days of having to match your shoes to your dress. While silk or satin shoes in the color of your gown are a classic choice, many brides today are choosing more colorful and fun options. Be sure to choose a pair that you can dance and stand in comfortably—remember, you'll be on your feet for hours.
- **Hosiery.** If you're wearing hosiery, go for the sheerest champagne, nude, or blush color you can find (depending on your dress color, sheer white or ivory are fine, too). Have an extra

pair handy on the big day in case of disasters just before the ceremony.

+ **Intimates.** You'll want undergarments that work specifically with your gown. These may include a strapless or push-up bra, a corset, special tummy-reducing underwear, and a slip or petticoat.

Man, Oh, Man!

Wedding attire is subject to the degree of formality, the season, and the time of day of the wedding. Most likely, the men will be wearing some form of tuxedo or suit. Though every tuxedo carries an air of formality, some are actually dressier than others. To brighten up a plain tuxedo, consider having the groomsmen wear vests and bow ties that match or complement the bridesmaids' dresses.

The Groom

As long as a groom knows the basics of the wedding details (how formal, which season, the hour), any formalwear shop will point him and his attendants in the right direction, while simultaneously steering him away from huge fashion errors. You wouldn't want your groom to arrive at your wedding completely overdressed (wearing a top hat at your beach wedding, for example), or way underdressed (wearing shorts in the cathedral).

If you're having a very informal wedding—on the beach or in a park, for instance—your groom may not need a tuxedo at all.

Weddings are basically categorized by their pageantry (things like the setting, your dress, the formality or informality of the reception site), and each style carries its own rules about appropriate apparel.

+ **Informal or semiformal wedding (daytime):** dark formal suit (in summer, select a lighter shade and fabric), white dress shirt, dress shoes, and dark socks

- **Semiformal wedding (evening):** formal suit or dinner jacket with matching trousers (preferably black), white shirt, cummerbund or vest, black bow tie, studs, and cuff links
- **Formal wedding (daytime):** cutaway or stroller jacket in gray or black, white high-collared (wing-collared) shirt, waistcoat (usually gray), striped trousers, striped tie or ascot, studs, and cuff links
- **Formal wedding (evening):** black dinner jacket and trousers, white tuxedo shirt, waistcoat, black four-in-hand tie, cummerbund, cuff links
- **Very formal wedding (daytime):** cutaway (black or gray), wing-collared shirt, vest, gray striped trousers, ascot, gloves, cuff links
- **Very formal wedding (evening):** black tailcoat, white pique shirt, white waistcoat, white bow tie, black trousers, patent leather shoes, studs, cuff links

The Groom's Attendants

In general, all the groomsmen dress the same as each other, in a style and color that complement the groom's outfit. Many men rent their formalwear these days. Your best bet is to have the men reserve their attire at least two to three months before the wedding. In the busy wedding months between April and October, formalwear may be hard to come by. If your wedding occurs during these months, make sure the guys look around and reserve things extra early.

Any male attendant who lives out of town should go to a reputable tuxedo shop in his area to be measured. Have the groomsman send the measurements to your fiancé so he can reserve the attire with the rest of the group's. Remember to ask your formalwear shop about exact prices, including alterations. Also, inquire about their return policy (including *when* to return the clothing).

GROOM'S ATTIRE WORKSHEET

TUXEDO SHOP

Name:
....

Address:
....

Telephone: .... Salesperson: ....

Store hours:
....

Directions:
....

....

Services included:
....

GROOM'S ATTIRE

Tuxedo style and color:
....

Cost: .... Order date: ....

Deposit paid: .... Date: ....

Balance due: .... Date: ....

Fitting date #1: .... Time: ....

Fitting date #2: .... Time: ....

Pick-up date and time:
....

Return date and time:
....

Late fee:
....

Terms of cancellation:
....

....

GROOM'S MEASUREMENTS

Groom's height: ....

Weight: ....

Coat size: ....

Arm inseam: ....

Pants waist: ....

Length (outseam): ....

Shirt neck: ....

Sleeve: ....

Shoe size: ....

Width: ....

Notes: ....

Accessory	Size	Color	Cost	Where Purchased (if different from above)	Picked Up?
Tie/Ascot:					
Cummerbund:					
Pocket handkerchief:					
Suspenders:					
Studs:					
Cuff links:					
Formal socks:					
Shoes:					
Top hat:					
Cane:					
Gloves:					
Other:					

Bridal Beauty

This is not the day to try to jump-start that new beehive hairdo trend you've been considering. Stick to what's been working for you all along. If you must try something new, give it a trial run (or two or three) well in advance of the big day.

Hair

If you're like many brides, you'll want to reach for the security of your stylist on your wedding day, either because you feel no one can make you look better or because your hands are too busy shaking to wield a brush.

Brides walking out of a salon, wearing an up-do, a veil, a shirt that buttons (because you can't pull a T-shirt over your perfectly groomed hair, after all), and jeans are a fairly common sight, especially during the busy wedding months. However, if you don't want to be seen in public this way, ask your hairdresser if it's possible for her to make the trip to your home (or wherever you'll be preparing for the ceremony). This might also save you the trouble of exposing your perfect hairdo to any nasty weather—a virtual guarantee of a bad hair day.

Makeup

Even if you're completely happy with your daily makeup selection and application skills, you may want to find something special for your wedding day. A department store cosmetologist will gladly give you a consultation and a makeover, especially if it impels you to buy some of her products. If you're impressed by her abilities and her advice, buy whatever items you want or need and go home and practice.

The alternative to a department store cosmetologist is a professional cosmetologist. She'll cost more, of course, but she won't be worried about selling you a specific line of cosmetics. She'll use whatever looks best on you (and she'll try to sell you that). This is the woman you can hire to come to your home before the wedding. If she does a great job, book her. She'll be worth every penny, and you can be confident that you'll look radiant not just throughout the day, but in all of those wedding photos as well.

For an inexpensive alternative for learning the latest tricks and trends of beauty, visit a site such as YouTube and search the topic you're interested in—say, "wedding day makeup." There are plenty of professional makeup artists and cosmetologists trying to make a name for themselves who post their "secrets"—if you have the attention span and the courage to try it yourself, go for it. But again, this is not something to try the day of your wedding. Give it a whirl at least a month in advance and perfect and personalize the steps from there.

Manicure

Perhaps you think that having someone file your nails and attend to your cuticles seems frivolous, but consider this: after admiring your dress, your hair, and your new husband, friends and family are going to want to see your ring finger, and people are going to want pictures of you modeling the ring. If your fingernails are misshapen, bitten, or just plain unattractive, consider salvaging them for this one day.

BRIDAL BEAUTY WORKSHEET

HAIRSTYLIST

NAME

Salon:

Address:

Telephone: Hours:

CONSULTATIONS

Date: Time:

Date: Time:

Date: Time:

WEDDING DAY APPOINTMENT

Location:

Date: Time: Number of hours:

Services included:

Total cost of services: Overtime cost:

MANICURIST/PEDICURIST

NAME

Salon:

Address:

Telephone: Hours:

WEDDING DAY APPOINTMENT

Location:

Date: Time: Number of hours:

Services included:

....

....

Total cost of services: Overtime cost:

....

MAKEUP ARTIST

NAME

Salon:

....

Address:

....

....

Telephone:

....

Hours:

CONSULTATIONS

Date: Time:

....

Date: Time:

....

Date: Time:

WEDDING DAY APPOINTMENT

Location:

....

Date: Time: Number of hours:

....

Services included:

....

....

Total cost of services: Overtime cost:

....

Travel fee *(if applicable)*:

....

Notes:

....

....

CHAPTER 9

The Ins and Outs of Receptions

A TYPICAL RECEPTION has finery, etiquette, cakes, and dances—and this is only a partial list. This chapter takes you on a ride through planning the big party.

Start Looking Now

The first thing you have to do is find a place to have your reception. Religious officiants will tell you to set the ceremony date first and then find a reception site. Many couples, however, try to do just the opposite. Of course, this is like the chicken-and-the-egg question. What it really comes down to is whether you are more particular about the site of the wedding ceremony or of the reception. If you just have to be married in the church your parents were married in, for example, and its available dates don't coincide with the dates available at the reception site you're considering, then you'll just have to find another reception location.

On the other hand, if you want your reception in a certain location, but the location of the actual ceremony doesn't really matter to you (you'll even consider a civil ceremony on the premises), your choice is obvious.

Your Reception Investigation

You can start your search for the ideal reception site by asking friends for their recommendations. Visit the places you're considering, go through all the questions listed in the "Who to Contact and What to Ask" section in this chapter, and write down the answers for easy comparison later on. Note carefully whether the people you will be dealing with are courteous and responsive to your wishes, too.

If you like a venue and the prices quoted, go back there to see a wedding or a formal dinner in progress, especially if you have never been to a function there. If you are considering a restaurant or a country club, it is a good idea to have dinner there on a Saturday or Sunday, when, presumably, the kitchen and waitstaff are putting forth their best efforts at their busiest time. Take note of the activity. Will your party have adequate privacy if the rest of the place is full? What kind of ambiance is projected by the setting, service, and clientele? Carefully check the maintenance of (and the lines forming near) the restrooms on a busy evening.

If a place seems like a good possibility, have the site manager give you a preliminary estimate in writing, spelling out the details of the menu, service, and everything else you've discussed. Then compare your various estimates and impressions before you commit to anything.

Who to Contact and What to Ask

Because reserving the reception site is a business transaction (not the most romantic way to think of your wedding day, but perhaps the most practical), you should treat your interview with the banquet manager as such. Here are some questions to ask:

- How many people can the facility comfortably seat? How big is the dance floor?
- Where does the receiving line typically form? Where is the gift table set up? What about the cake table?
- Is in-house catering available? Can you bring in your own caterer?
- How many hours is the site available? Is there a minimum amount of time you must reserve? Are there charges if the reception runs over?
- Is there free parking? If there is valet parking, what are the rates and gratuities?
- Will there be coatroom and restroom attendants? A bartender? A doorman? What are the charges for each?

Check out the reception hall when a reception is underway, and record your observations to the following questions:

Overall impression?

....

....

....

....

....

Is the dance floor an adequate size?

....

....

....

....

....

Is the flow of people moving smoothly? Are there any bottlenecks around doors or hallways?

....

....

....

....

Does the reception site have all the furniture (tables, chairs, buffet areas, stage for band or DJ, etc.) you will need?

....

....

....

....

....

Is the meal or buffet served all at once or are some people waiting for their food?

....

....

....

....

....

Is the bar running smoothly?

....

....

....

....

....

Is the noise at an acceptable level?

....

....

....

....

....

Do people appear to be enjoying themselves?

....

....

....

....

....

....

- If you're opting for food stations, where are they set up?
- If there isn't a bar, where can your caterer set up his or her bar?
- If you've arranged for an open bar, are there any limits as to what kinds of alcohol will be served? If you've arranged for a cash bar, what will the prices be?
- Does the facility have more than one reception room on the premises? Is yours the only reception scheduled that day, or is there one before or after (or at the same time in another room)?
- What are the cancellation policies? Is the deposit refundable?
- Is there a printed layout of the facility available for your planning purposes?

Ask to see the kitchen, even if you're bringing in your own caterer. If it's not spick-and-span, think about going elsewhere, no matter how much you love the reception area.

There are other issues to discuss as well, such as where your musicians will set up, how and where your decorations will be displayed, and how many guests will be seated at each table.

That Costs How Much?

Make sure you're aware of all reception-related charges up front. A deposit (usually a great big one) will reserve the site you want. Many sites won't refund this deposit if you decide you don't want to use the facility. Before you sign on the dotted line, get references from previous clients (yes, it takes some time, but you're protecting your potential investment), and review the agreement carefully. As always, make sure every part of your final negotiations, including date, time, services, and policies, is in writing.

Sales tax, an item sometimes overlooked, adds a hefty amount to the already large reception cost. Cancellations, changes, and last-minute additions may also cost additional money. You don't want to come home sunburned and (happily) exhausted from your

RECEPTION SITE WORKSHEET

Reception site:

....

Address:

....

Telephone:

....

Contact: Website:

APPOINTMENTS

Date: Time:

....

Date: Time:

....

Date: Time:

....

Date: Time:

COST

Total amount due:

....

Amount of deposit: Date:

....

Balance due: Date:

....

Room reserved:

....

Date: Time: Number of hours:

....

Overtime cost:

....

Occupancy:

Final head count due date:

....

Reception location includes the following services:

....

....

Reception location includes the following equipment:

....

....

Terms of cancellation:

....

....

Other:

....

Item:	Description:	Cost:	Notes:

RECEPTION SITE

Site rental:

....

Overtime fee:

....

Other:

EQUIPMENT

Tent:

....

Chairs:

....

Tables:

....

Linens:

....

Other:

SERVICE

Servers:

....

Bartenders:

....

Valet parking
   attendants:

....

Coat checkers:

....

Other:

OTHER (LIST BELOW)

....

....

Total: _____

honeymoon only to discover that your wedding money will go toward paying the hidden fees associated with the reception.

Receiving Your Guests

The present-day etiquette for receiving lines is short and sweet: You should definitely have one (guests tend to feel slighted or ignored if you opt to skip out on your duty of saying hello to each and every one of them), but keep it simple. The order of the line is not even terribly structured these days. As long as you include the essential players, you're in good standing. Your attendants do not have to be included in your receiving line, and honestly, your Aunt Sue probably doesn't care one way or the other about saying hello to your new husband's college roommate who is serving as groomsman number eight. Typically, the line consists of the newlyweds, the parents of the bride and groom, and the honor attendants (who can serve double duty as go-fers during this time. Feel free to say, "I'm so thirsty from saying hello to so many people. Would you please grab me a glass of water?").

The receiving line should form after the ceremony but before the reception. If you're not worried about the line taking up too much time on your big day, or if you and your groom are not immediately proceeding to the reception (because you're taking photos, for example), try to have the receiving line at the wedding site.

If you elect that option, be sure to check with your officiant first. Some churches and synagogues have restrictions concerning where the line may be formed. The most convenient spot is often near an exit or outside, where guests can move through easily on their way to the reception. If you choose to have the line at the reception site, have refreshments and entertainment available for guests while they're waiting.

If a guest is a complete stranger to you, introduce yourself. Be friendly but brief. A simple "Thank you so much for coming! It's so good to see you!" or, "I've heard so much about you," in the case of meeting new relations for the first time will suffice. Should one guest monopolize your time, hand them off to your maid of honor by saying, "Mrs. Smith, this is my very best friend, Amy; she'll show you where to put your coat and help you find the bar."

The Seating Chart

Unless you're planning a cocktail reception with hors d'oeuvres or an informal buffet, you're going to need a seating chart. Guests (especially those who don't know many people) often feel uncomfortable without assigned seating.

Placing People

If you're planning a very formal wedding, place cards are necessary for all guests. At less formal receptions, place cards are used only at the head table. The easiest way to alert guests to their table assignments is to place table cards on a table near the reception room entrance. Table cards simply list the name of the guest and their table assignment. Another option is to set up an enlarged seating diagram at the reception entrance.

Save Me a Seat!

The head table is wherever the bride and groom sit, and is, understandably, the focus of the reception. This table usually faces the other tables. Sometimes the table is placed on a platform, and decorations are kept low so guests can see you and your groom kissing and gazing into each other's eyes—even as you scarf down your filet mignon.

Traditionally, the bride and groom, honor attendants, bridesmaids, and groomsmen sit at the head table. The bride and groom sit in the middle, with the best man next to the bride and the maid of honor next to the groom. (The seating of the attendants should alternate male-female around the table from there.)

You may also choose to have a table for two—just you and your groom. Or you could sit with your honor attendants at the head table and seat the rest of your attendants together at a smaller table.

The Parents and Officiant

Parents of the bride and groom usually sit at separate tables with their own families. Still, there's no single correct seating arrangement for the parents' tables. The bride and groom's parents can sit together with the officiant, or each set of parents can host their own table with family and friends.

The officiant should be seated in a place of honor at the reception. Make sure that one of the parents' tables includes the officiant and his or her spouse. Seating the person who pronounced you husband and wife near the kitchen or the back door is a no-no.

Not-So-Musical Chairs

Where do you seat your divorced, actively warring parents? As far away from each other as possible without offending either of them. The trick here is to place them at separate tables that are in the vicinity of the head table, but not so close to each other that they'll have to hear their ex-spouse's voice.

Here's a scenario. If your groom's parents are not divorced, you could reserve three tables in front of the head table for seating the parents—one for your mom and her family, one for your groom's parents, and one for your dad and his family. Your in-laws' table would be smack dab in the middle in this setup—neutral territory.

SEATING CHART WORKSHEET

HEAD TABLE

Shape of table:
....

Number of chairs:
....

Order of seating (list or draw diagram below):
....

....

....

....

BRIDE'S PARENTS' TABLE

Shape of table:
....

Number of chairs:
....

Order of seating (list or draw diagram below):
....

....

....

....

....

GROOM'S PARENTS' TABLE

Shape of table:
....

Number of chairs:
....

Order of seating (list or draw diagram below):
....

....

....

....

....

GUEST TABLES

Shape of tables:

....

Average number of chairs per table:

....

Total number of guests:

....

Table number _____

Name of guest:

....

....

....

....

....

....

....

....

Table number _____

Name of guest:

....

....

....

....

....

....

....

....

Table number _____   Table number _____

Name of guest: Name of guest:
....
....
....
....
....
....
....

Table number _____   Table number _____

Name of guest: Name of guest:
....
....
....
....
....
....
....

Table number _____   Table number _____

Name of guest: Name of guest:
....
....
....
....
....
....
....

SEATING CHART WORKSHEET (CONTINUED)

Table number _____

Name of guest:
....
....
....
....
....
....
....

Table number _____

Name of guest:
....
....
....
....
....
....
....

Table number _____

Name of guest:
....
....
....
....
....
....
....

Table number _____

Name of guest:
....
....
....
....
....
....
....

Table number _____

Name of guest:
....
....
....
....
....
....
....

Table number _____

Name of guest:
....
....
....
....
....
....
....

Events During the Reception

You're probably already familiar with the traditions of the first toast, the first dance, the cake-cutting, and the bouquet and garter throwing. But just in case you're a little foggy on them (or still up in the air over whether to include them in your reception), here's a refresher.

Toasts

Brides rarely give toasts at their own weddings, though they certainly can if they're so inclined. Best men are the first in line to present a toast. However, many young men aren't well versed in wedding etiquette. You or your fiancé may need to give your best man a few pointers—such as less is always more, and risqué commentary has no place in a room full of elderly relatives.

The recipient of a toast does not drink at the end of the salute, but simply smiles at the person offering the kind words. The maid of honor, the bride or groom's parents, and your siblings or close friends may all make toasts if they wish. All toasts except the best man's toast are optional. Once the toasting is over, the dinner is served, and your best man can stop his profuse perspiring. His duties have been met.

Opening Dances

The newlyweds' first dance is often one of the most romantic parts of your reception. You and your new partner will dance to a song the two of you have carefully chosen for its message of undying love while your guests look on and smile.

After the first dance, the bride dances with her father, and then the groom dances with his mother. Afterward, the bride and groom's parents dance, the bride dances with her new father-in-law, the groom dances with his new mother-in-law, and the bridesmaids and groomsmen dance with each other.

Feel free to eliminate or combine some or all of these dances, and when you're ready to mambo with the masses, have the DJ, bandleader, or master of ceremonies announce when everyone is welcome on the dance floor.

The Cake-Cutting Ceremony

Aside from being a tasty little treat, the wedding cake performs a very important function as the centerpiece of the cake-cutting ceremony, when the bride and groom cut the first piece of cake together and feed each other a bite as the crowd watches to see whether either of you has the guts to smash the other one's face with it. At a sit-down reception, the cake is usually cut right before the dessert, if any, is served. However, if you have a photographer who is trying to move things along, don't be surprised if he or she wants to move the cake-cutting up a bit. The caterer will cut the rest of the cake and distribute it to the guests.

Other Events

There are other events that couples opt for—the garter and bouquet toss, for example, or the dollar dance, or the limbo. Some activities have fallen out of favor and the newly married couple wouldn't be caught dead participating in them, while some have gained kitsch status and couples do everything in their power to include them in the reception. Don't feel pressured to include any event that you and your groom wouldn't enjoy on your wedding day.

Outdoor Receptions

Receptions in the great big arms of Mother Nature are becoming more and more commonplace these days. Whether the party takes place in a park, a vineyard, or your own backyard, there are a few things you might want to consider:

- **Do not plan this event in a devil-may-care fashion.** Outdoor events take an extra step of planning because of the possibility of inclement weather. Go ahead and rent the tent, even if you have a hunch it's going to be sunny and mild on your big day. You just never know, and some of your guests will prefer to sit in the shade, anyway.

- **Get as formal or as creative as you want.** Unlike indoor receptions, where the level of formality is dictated by the venue itself, the great outdoors gives you the freedom to have any kind of wedding you want—you can go ultra-high-class or host a barefoot barbecue.

- **Inform your guests that they will be outdoors.** If you're getting married under a grand oak tree in the state park, for example, your female guests will not want to wear their stiletto heels, which will sink into the grass.

- **Set a mood.** If you're hosting a reception in your own backyard, for example, transform the place for a day. Throw twinkling lights over anything that will stand still—trees, fences, shrubbery. Wrap tulle around the chairs in the yard; fire up the tiki torches. Inexpensive doesn't have to mean dull!

- **Don't forget the music.** Even if you're gathering just twelve people around the pool for a tiny reception, prepare a playlist for them to groove and celebrate to. It makes the day more special, and adds to your memories.

RECEPTION EVENTS WORKSHEET

Give a copy of this checklist to your reception site coordinator and band leader or disc jockey.

Introduce entire
  bridal party?   ◯ Yes   ◯ No   Music:
....

Introduce only
  bride and groom?   ◯ Yes   ◯ No   Music:
....

Parent(s) of bride:
....

Parent(s) of groom:
....

Grandparent(s) of bride:
....

Grandparent(s) of groom:
....

Flower girl(s):
....

Ringbearer(s):
....

Bridesmaids: Ushers:
....

....

....

....

....

Maid of honor: Best man:
....

Matron of honor:
....

Bride's first name: Groom's first name:
....

Bride and groom as they
  are to be introduced:
....

Receiving line
   at reception?   ○ Yes   ○ No   When:
....

                          Music:
....

Blessing?   ○ Yes   ○ No   By whom:
....

First toast?   ○ Yes   ○ No   By whom:
....

Other toasts?   ○ Yes   ○ No   By whom:
....

                          By whom:
....

                          By whom:
....

First dance: ○ Yes   ○ No   When:
....

                          Music:
....

To join in first dance:
....

Maid of honor
   and best man?   ○ Yes   ○ No
....

Parents of bride
   and groom?   ○ Yes   ○ No
....

Bridesmaids and ushers?   ○ Yes   ○ No
....

Guests?   ○ Yes   ○ No
....

Father-daughter dance?   ○ Yes   ○ No   Music:
....

Mother-son dance?   ○ Yes   ○ No   Music:
....

Open dance floor for
   guests after first dance? ○ Yes   ○ No
....

Cake cutting?   ○ Yes   ○ No   Music:
....

Bouquet toss?   ○ Yes   ○ No
....

Garter toss?   ○ Yes ○ No

Last dance?   ○ Yes ○ No   Music:

Other event:

When: Music:

Other event:

When: Music:

Special requests and dedications:

Notes:

CHAPTER 10

Food, Glorious (Catered) Food

ALTHOUGH YOU AND YOUR GROOM will probably be too excited and too busy to eat much on your wedding day, it would be wrong to assume the same about your guests. The two of you will be feasting on love and champagne. Your guests, on the other hand, will probably be looking forward to beef, chicken, shrimp, a sandwich—anything, in short, to stave off starvation. That's where the caterer comes in.

Finding a Caterer

Along with your budget, the type and location of your reception will help you determine the kind of caterer you need. After that, all that's left is to find out who can feed your guests best at a price you can afford.

In-House Caterers

If you're lucky, your reception site will have an in-house caterer who fits your budget, serves great food, and knows how to work with you. There are several advantages to using an in-house caterer, the biggest being that you don't have to go through the trouble of finding one yourself. These folks are already familiar with the particulars of the room, which itself is a perk with many advantages. For instance, linens and dinnerware that complement the overall atmosphere are already in rotation, and the waitstaff have already carefully choreographed their serving routine.

Unfortunately, in-house catering is usually more expensive than independent catering, often charging you for lots of little extras (things you may not want or need) as part of one all-inclusive package. Some reception places with on-site caterers may allow you the option of bringing in another catering service, but most likely, it's their way or the highway. If the food is good and the price is just a little on the high side, you might find that this arrangement is worth the money simply because it's so convenient.

Independent Caterers

Finding an independent food-and-drink team is actually fairly easy. The good ones sell themselves by word of mouth (ask any business manager or event planner, or even a friend who entertains regularly, for their recommendations), and there are always fresh upstarts in this business who are eager to show off their wares. The one downside is that catering is fairly expensive—and that makes sense. You're paying someone to cook, serve, and clean up after your guests, which is no small feat.

Before you go searching for an independent caterer, find out what your reception site provides and what it doesn't. Some sites offer linens, glass and dinnerware, tables, chairs—everything but the food. Others provide nothing but the space. Know what you need before you go looking for an independent caterer.

Bare-bones caterers specialize in keeping it simple. They provide food, and that's it. Everything else—beverages, linens, dinnerware, glasses, even waiters and waitresses—is left completely up to you. Sometimes this can work to your advantage. Caterers like these may offer great food at a low price, and you may be able to find a good deal on everything else that you'll need. You can save quite a bit of money this way. If you purchase alcohol in quantity, for instance, you'll avoid the outrageous markups that usually accompany liquor provided by caterers.

The disadvantage, of course, is the inconvenience. If your reception site doesn't provide tables and chairs, for example, you'll have to research what you'll need and determine a fair price for the cost of any rentals. Then you'll have to orchestrate getting everything to the site on your wedding day and returning it. The task is not impossible, but it may require more work than you initially think.

Full-service caterers, which most people associate with a wedding reception, provide food, beverages, waitstaff, and bartenders. Most also offer linens and dinnerware. If you need tables and chairs, these caterers will usually do all the legwork for you and simply add that to your bill. If you're lucky, they'll charge you exactly what the rental agency charged them. It's not uncommon for caterers to add a fee for their trouble, so get a written estimate before you authorize anything. Some of these caterers will let you supply the alcohol, but others prefer not to worry about the potential liability (or their loss of liquor revenue).

Then there are the caterers that offer just about every item and service you could imagine, and a few you probably couldn't. Many of these caterers have branched out into the reception-coordinating business. If you choose to pay them for it, they'll take on the entire responsibility of planning your reception, including music, flowers, photographer—the whole nine yards. This may sound like a dream come true, but unless you're careful, it has the potential to become quite a nightmare.

First, there is the cost. This kind of service doesn't come cheap. Second, you're flying blind. How are you to know whether you'll get a high-quality photographer or some close (amateur) friend of the coordinator who happens to have a nice camera? Third and most important is the question of quality. With so many irons in so many fires, even seasoned veterans can make mistakes. If you find such a catering service that really appeals to you, consider contracting them for the traditional catering services—but keep a tight rein on everything else.

One last tip: even if you ask for recommendations from friends, relatives, and business associates, do not hire a caterer until you have sampled the very food you plan on serving to your guests. Any caterer worth their salt will offer you samples at a cut rate, so don't hesitate to ask.

Questions to Ask the Caterer

No matter what type of caterer you choose, you'll need to ask a lot of questions to make sure that they can provide the services you're looking for. Don't play the part of the shy bride during this interview—your wedding (and your hard-earned money) lies in the balance. You don't want to kick yourself later for not asking a relatively obvious question when you had the chance.

The Cost

You'll want to know about the price of the food. Caterers can give you an estimate based on current food prices. Closer to the wedding, they should be able to give you the final price, reflecting the prices at that time. Ask about how much of a difference you should expect. For instance, you don't want to end up paying $50 for a meal if the estimate you're given initially is $25. You should also ask about price guarantees.

You'll want to know if your overall estimate includes meals for your disc jockey (or an entire band), your photographer, your videographer, and anyone else you'll have on the clock that evening. Also, ask whether the cost covers gratuities for the staff and the cost of the bartender, coatroom attendant, and anyone else who will be working at your reception.

Don't forget to ask about the refund policy. It's not a pleasant topic to broach, but what if, for example, a hurricane blew into town on the same weekend as your wedding? Or what if you and your fiancé decide next week that you're going to elope? What will happen to your down payment? Will you be held responsible for any additional payments?

The Food

No matter how simple or fancy the service, you want to know whether this caterer can meet your needs. Ask if there are different options. Can your guests choose between fish (a popular choice lately) or red meat (always popular)? If you have vegetarian or kosher guests attending the reception, can special meals be prepared for them? What about the wedding cake? Can this caterer provide one, or will you need a baker on the side?

What about the leftover food? In the past, folks frowned on their hosts taking that food home. Now it's more commonplace to see a caterer wrap up any extra meals—and considering what you're likely to pay for those meals, you shouldn't feel funny about asking about this option. Another idea is to have those meals donated to a local soup kitchen or shelter.

The Contract

When you decide on a caterer who meets your budget and who has answered these questions to your satisfaction, *get every part of your agreement in writing*. Don't leave any stone unturned—you might get tripped up later. If you're not familiar with a caterer's work, or if he or she is new to the business, ask for references— the names of those who have used their services recently. This is critically important when you're planning almost a year ahead. You'll be asked to give a sizable deposit, and you want to make sure the caterer will still be in business when the date arrives!

Sit-Down, Buffet, or Stations?

You'll hear opinions from everyone on these issues, and every opinion will be different. Your mom will prefer a buffet meal because it's less expensive, but your newly married friend might tell you that buffet foods taste like warmed-up leftovers. How's a bride to choose?

Choosing the Menu

If you're working with an on-site caterer, your choices will most likely be laid out for you with little to no variation in them— and that's all right, because these selections tend to be crowd-friendly. There's a little something for everyone, and nothing that's particularly offbeat. One tip, however: when you meet with the catering manager, ask him or her point-blank which dishes he or she would recommend and why. Do not phrase this question as, "What's good on this menu?" as the response will likely be, "Oh, it's all wonderful!" No, no, no. You want to know what the on-site cook/chef does particularly well.

As far as cost is concerned, chicken is less expensive than beef. What's more, chicken (as long as it's not fried or wrapped in bacon) is the healthier option. In this age of diet and health awareness, many people simply don't eat much red meat anymore.

On the other hand, some hosts (your parents, for example) may feel they're being cheap if they don't serve beef, although it's doubtful that the choice will make or break your wedding. If you're really concerned, offer your guests a choice of several meals. On their response card, give them the option of checking off poultry or beef (or fish, or vegetarian—whatever you have worked out with your caterer).

There are also caterers who specialize in menus for specific diets. If you're a vegan or are on a special diet such as gluten- or lactose-free, try investigating caterers who work entirely with that kind of menu. A simple Internet search can reveal some options, but never underestimate the power of word of mouth. Have a vegan restaurant that you love to frequent? Check to see if they provide catering services—many restaurants offer this service, or may be willing to work with you, since you're such a devoted and loyal customer. More on special diets later, but it could be safer to use someone who works with your ideal menu rather than hope another caterer can fake it.

Sit Down? Line Up?

There's a bit more to consider in the sit-down versus buffet debate. A sit-down meal is generally considered more formal than a buffet. In addition, many people feel they're treating their guests better by not making them stand in line for their food. Buffet service does have its advantages, though. Because it eliminates the need for an entire army of waiters and waitresses, it's usually less expensive to serve than a sit-down meal. A buffet can also add a relaxed touch to a morning or afternoon wedding.

If you decide to go with a buffet, consider having two lines instead of one. Your guests will get to the food twice as fast, an especially nice touch if you're planning a rather large wedding. Though a buffet service saves you the cost of waitstaff, it does require more food than a sit-down meal, because portions are not controlled. You will want to have plenty of food visible so that no one will feel shy about taking enough to eat. The caterer should assign a few staff members to watch the table and replace any food that starts to run low.

Semi-buffet service is another option. With this service, the tables are already set with plates, flatware, and glasses. The waitstaff clears the tables and serves drinks; the only thing the guests pick up at the buffet table is the food.

Stations

This option is gaining popularity with the buffet crowd. Rather than presenting your guests with warming trays of food, which could start to look unappetizing once the bulk of the line has attacked, this option calls for several manned food stations to be set up around the reception hall. Some common types of stations include a pasta station, a meat-carving station, or even a skewer station.

Salads, fresh fruit, steamed vegetables, breads and rolls, and other side dishes can be laid out on a separate table and self-served with plates provided. Tables are set with silverware and linens so guests only have to carry their plate of food. Condiments that complement the pasta, meats, or skewers, such as grated cheese, cranberry sauce, and au jus, should be placed near the items they accompany, but far enough away so that the line moves steadily along.

Special Diets and Food Allergies

Certain diets are not always a choice—you or your fiancé, or some of your guests, may be subject to a specific method of eating for health reasons. Someone may have celiac disease, which prevents them from properly digesting gluten, a wheat substance found in many foods including cake and bread; diabetes, which affects the body's processing of sugar; or lactose intolerance, an inability to ingest dairy products. More serious conditions may include food allergies, many of which can easily be avoided by not eating certain foods, but others can be more critical—for example, sufferers of peanut allergies can be severely affected by the mere presence of a peanut product in their vicinity. While you don't have to run a medical history on every one of your guests, it might be a good idea to think about any dietary restrictions that might be an issue.

You may wish to have a menu that reflects some of these types of diets, or at least include an option or two that these guests or attendees can select. Check with your caterer, or ask if these options are possible with potential caterers. If a guest reaches out to you before the wedding and asks about his or her dietary options, or you bring it up with your caterer, there is almost always a (delicious) solution that can be reached.

Liquor: Cash or Open Bar?

One of the hottest topics surrounding any wedding is whether to host a cash bar or an open bar. At the open bar, guests drink for free, courtesy of you or whoever is footing the bill. At a cash bar, they have to pony up for their own drinks. Some people will suggest to you that it's rude to expect your guests to pay for their own drinks. After all, you wouldn't normally host a party and expect your guests to pay for what you serve them.

The other side of the debate is the fact that open bars can end up being extremely expensive. People are often wasteful with liquor that they haven't paid for. Someone might order a drink, take a sip, and go off to the powder room. The drink is forgotten, or the guest assumes it's gotten warm and orders a fresh one. Besides, why shouldn't this guest take full advantage of your generosity?

Other Options

If you really don't want to make your guests buy drinks, there are a few options that might work for you:

◆ Have an open bar for the first hour of the reception only. This will ease your guilt, help your guests pass the time pleasantly while you're off taking pictures, and minimize any problems with guests.

◆ Serve free champagne punch. A punch like this is fairly light, in terms of alcohol content, and people aren't likely to pound down glass after glass.

◆ Place bottles of wine on the tables. A typical bottle of wine holds four to five servings. At a table seated for eight, a bottle of red and a bottle of white ensures that everyone gets a glass or two of wine with their meal.

If your reception site allows it, you may be able to save some money by purchasing a few kegs or several cases of high-quality beer plus some cases of good wine. Offer other alcohol or cocktails for cash for those who prefer something harder.

Feed the Masses Yourself

Brides who plan smallish weddings can sometimes get away with feeding the guests themselves. One word of warning: this requires extensive planning and a lot of help. If you have doubts about preparing and setting up food for your guests in the hours preceding your wedding, look for a caterer who offers the just-food (no service) option. You'll be much happier to have shelled out a few hundred dollars and saved your sanity.

At a very relaxed reception, feeding your guests yourself is doable and will save you a lot of money, but make it easy on yourself: Make it a family-style or buffet event. Plan a menu that's easy to prepare in bulk: ziti, stuffed shells, sliced ham, salad, rolls.

CATERER WORKSHEET

Name *(if different from reception site)*:
....

Address:
....

....

Telephone:
....

Contact: Hours:

Date: Time:
....

Date: Time:
....

Date: Time:
....

Date of hired services: Time:

Number of hours: Cocktail hour:
....

Overtime cost: Final head count due date:
....

Menu:
....

....

....

Sit-down or buffet?
....

Includes the following services:
....

....

Includes the following equipment:
....

COST

Total amount due:
....

Amount of deposit: Date:
....

Balance due: Date:
....

Gratuities included? ◯ Yes ◯ No   Sales tax included? ◯ Yes ◯ No

Terms of cancellation:
....

Notes:
....

....

CATERER WORKSHEET (CONTINUED)

Item	Description	Cost	Notes
FOOD			
Appetizers			
Entrées			
Dessert			
Other food			
BEVERAGES			
Nonalcoholic			
Champagne			
Wine			
Liquor			
EQUIPMENT			
Tent			
Chairs			
Tables			
Linens			
Dinnerware			
Flatware			
Glassware			
Serving pieces			
Other			
SERVICE			
Servers			
Bartenders			
Valet parking attendants			
Coat checkers			
Overtime cost			
OTHER			

Gratuities _____   **Sales tax** _____   TOTAL _____

FOOD AND BEVERAGE WORKSHEET

Food	Description	Number	Cost
Appetizers			
Entrées			
Desserts *(if any)*			
Beverages *(nonalcoholic)*			
Wine			
Champagne			
Open bar			
Other			
Gratuities			
Sales tax			
TOTAL			

EQUIPMENT RENTAL WORKSHEET

Name of rental company:
....

Address:
....

....

Telephone:
....

Contact:
....

Hours:
....

Order date:
....

Delivery? Pick up? *(circle one)*
....

Date: Time:
....

Special instructions:
....

Total amount due:
....

Amount of deposit: Date:
....

Balance due: Date:
....

Cancellation policy:
....

....

....

Damaged goods policy:
....

....

....

Notes:
....

....

....

....

....

....

CHAPTER 11

By Invitation Only

ALTHOUGH NINE OUT OF TEN PEOPLE you'll invite to your wedding will probably already know the date, time, and place, you still have to send out invitations. Some people need something to stick on the refrigerator as a reminder of the upcoming event. Sending out invitations is also a good way to keep track of who's coming and who's not, provided people pay attention to your RSVP.

Choosing Invitations

The look of your invitation gives people their first impression of the type of wedding you'll be having. If you send out invitations that proclaim "We're Getting Hitched!" it's doubtful that your guests will expect a formal affair with top hats and tails. Make sure you choose invitations that are appropriate for the occasion you're planning.

The Old-Fashioned Method

Many brides still find their invitations by going to a designated stationery store and browsing through the catalogs. These catalogs contain samples of predesigned invitations—the paper color, paper stock, borders, and ornamentation have already been set. You pick out the color of the paper and ink, the style of the script, and the words you want to use. Many invitations come complete with phrasing. All you do is supply the specific information for your wedding, and the manufacturer does the rest.

These sample catalogs are created by a handful of large printing companies that dominate the invitation market. By printing several lines of mass-produced invitations, these companies are able to offer a greater variety and a lower price than a private company. Because these companies are a main manufacturer of wedding invitations, you'll probably see the same sample catalogs in the majority of places you look.

The Internet

Countless websites sell traditional and unique invitations, and if you're looking for a real bargain, you'll find it here. The downside, of course, is that you're taking a chance. Many brides like to see and feel their prospective invitations. (Is the paper heavy enough? Is the lettering raised enough? Are the die cuts crisp enough?) If you receive a box of 200 invitations that turn out to be very flimsy, you'll instantly regret this choice. One way to prevent an error like this is to educate yourself in matters such as paper stock and the various printing methods—and read online reviews of the final products. Obviously, the vendor itself will only list the best reviews on their site, so do a more general search. Plug the vendor's name in your favorite search engine followed by the word *reviews*, and make sure that the resulting pages are not hosted or owned by the vendor itself.

Once you have found a reliable source for them, ordering online invitations is an excellent way to create personalized and inexpensive invitations. And most orders can be processed within a week, so if you're short on time, this may be your best option.

A Personal Stationer

If you can't find an invitation you like online or in a stationery store, or if you want something very specific, there are private printers out there who can do the job for you. They may be a bit harder to find and more expensive than the big guys, but if you want your invitations to feature embossed lions on roller skates instead of the traditional doves and bells (hey, they're your invitations), private stationers might be your best bet. Look for local printers online.

Invitation Extras

Like the invitations themselves, the envelopes you choose can range from simple, with plain, high-quality paper, to fancy, with foil-laminated inner flaps or flaps with a colorful design. Beautifully packaged invitations are a nice touch, but as you might expect, the more you add, the greater the cost.

Plan to have the return address preprinted on the outer envelope and on the response cards. Traditionally, whoever is listed as the host for the wedding receives the RSVPs—but if you're the one communicating with the reception coordinator or caterer (even though your parents are the actual hosts) you might prefer to have the responses sent directly to you.

If the reception is at a different location than the ceremony, you will need to include a reception card in your invitations. Remember to include the full address of the reception site for the out-of-town guests. If dinner will be served, make it clear. You'll also need to include response cards. These are the cards that the guests send back to you so that you can add them to (or scratch them from) your final list.

What's the Word on Virtual Invites?

Here's the straight scoop: Etiquette mavens frown on the practice of sending electronic invitations for formal weddings; however, for brides who feel strongly about minimizing their carbon footprint, sending online invitations is an appealing option. (And let's be honest—electronic invites don't only save trees; they can also save couples a whole lot of cash.)

There are a few things to watch for:

- If you're planning a lavish affair, send paper invitations. Your guests will expect them, and sending an invitation via e-mail will simply seem tacky.
- Be aware of guests who may not have regular access to computers or e-mail, and therefore may not receive an electronic invitation in a timely manner. If you know, for example, that your Great Aunt Mae doesn't use a computer, send her a written invitation.

If you send virtual invitations and haven't heard back from certain prospective guests, go ahead and follow up with them.

Many people have their spam filters set to snag anything that doesn't come from an already established contact; it's possible that your invitation ended up in a junk folder somewhere.

What Are You Saying?

Having trouble figuring out how to word your invitations? You're not alone. With all of the mixed families in the world today, many brides find themselves wondering how the heck to print invitations without offending anyone. But you can relax—there are as many options for wording as there are for invitations.

Formal or Traditional

When the bride's parents are hosting the wedding:

Mr. and Mrs. Roger Parker
request the honor of your presence
at the marriage of their daughter
Elizabeth Elaine
to
Mr. Justin Clark
on Saturday, the second of August
Two thousand and seventeen
at two o'clock in the afternoon
Fairview Baptist Church
Fairview, Pennsylvania

When both the bride's and the groom's parents are hosting the wedding:

Mr. and Mrs. Roger Parker
and
Mr. and Mrs. Robert Clark
request the honor of your presence
at the marriage of their children
Elizabeth Elaine
and
Justin James
on Saturday, the fifth of August
Two thousand and seventeen
at two o'clock in the afternoon
Fairview Baptist Church
Fairview, Pennsylvania

Mr. and Mrs. Roger Parker
request the honor of your presence
at the marriage of their daughter
Elizabeth Elaine Parker
to
Justin James Clark
son of Mr. and Mrs. Robert Clark
Saturday, the fifth of August
Two thousand and seventeen
at two o'clock in the afternoon
Fairview Baptist Church
Fairview, Pennsylvania

When the groom's parents are hosting the wedding:

Mr. and Mrs. Robert Clark
request the honor of your presence
at the marriage of
Miss Elizabeth Elaine Parker
to their son
Mr. Justin James Clark

When the bride and groom are hosting their own wedding:

The honor of your presence is requested
at the marriage of
Miss Elizabeth Elaine Parker
and
Mr. Justin James Clark

Miss Elizabeth Elaine Parker
and
Mr. Justin James Clark
request the honor of your presence
at their marriage

Note that in all cases you should spell everything out—names, the year, the word *street*, and so on. It's all right to abbreviate common titles (such as Mr. and Mrs., for example), and it's also fine to use the numerical representations for the address of the church or synagogue, but only if you must. Generally, the address (including the street name) of the church can be omitted altogether, unless doing so will cause extreme amounts of anxiety for your guests (if, for example, you're getting married in New York City and no one would know *which* St. Andrew's you've chosen for your wedding site). If your entire guest list knows your hometown area well, you can simply opt for the name of the church (for example, St. Paul's Roman Catholic Church), followed by the town on the next line (Bedford, Illinois). Zip codes are *never* included.

Divorced Hosts

Circumstances will probably vary when divorced parents host a wedding. Use these examples as general guidelines.

When the mother of the bride is hosting and has not remarried:

Mrs. James Parker
requests the honor of your presence
at the marriage of her daughter
Elizabeth Elaine

When the mother of the bride is hosting and has remarried:

Mrs. David C. Hayes
requests the honor of your presence
at the marriage of her daughter
Elizabeth Elaine Parker

Mr. and Mrs. David C. Hayes
request the honor of your presence
at the marriage of Mrs. Hayes' daughter
Elizabeth Elaine Parker

When the father of the bride is hosting and has not remarried:

Mr. Roger Parker
requests the honor of your presence
at the marriage of his daughter
Elizabeth Elaine

When the father of the bride is hosting and has remarried:

Mr. and Mrs. Roger Parker
request the honor of your presence
at the marriage of Mr. Parker's daughter
Elizabeth Elaine

Deceased Parents

Deceased parents are usually not mentioned on wedding invitations because only the hosts of the event are listed. However, if you want to mention a late mother or father, no one is going to fault you for it.

When one parent is deceased and the host has not remarried:

Mrs. Ann Parker
requests the honor of your presence
at the marriage of her daughter
Elizabeth Elaine

Mrs. Ann Parker
requests the honor of your presence at the marriage of
Elizabeth Elaine,
daughter of Mrs. Parker and the late Roger Parker

When one parent is deceased and the host has remarried:

Mr. and Mrs. David Spencer
request the honor of your presence
at the marriage of Mrs. Spencer's daughter
Elizabeth Elaine

When both parents are deceased, and a close friend or relative is hosting:

Mr. and Mrs. Frederick Parker
request the honor of your presence
at the marriage of their granddaughter
Elizabeth Elaine Parker

Religious Ceremonies

The following are general guidelines for those who wish to emphasize the religious aspect of marriage. If you have any questions, consult your officiant before having the invitations printed.

For Protestant ceremonies:

Mr. and Mrs. Parker
are pleased to invite you
to join in a Christian celebration
of the marriage of their daughter Elizabeth Elaine Parker
to
Justin James Clark
on Saturday, the fifth of August
Two thousand seventeen
at ten o'clock in the morning
St. Phillip's Methodist Church
Fairview, Pennsylvania

For Catholic ceremonies:

Mr. and Mrs. Roger Parker
request the honor of your presence
at the Nuptial Mass
at which their daughter
Elizabeth Elaine
and
Justin James Clark
will be united in the
Sacrament of Holy Matrimony
on Saturday, the fifth of August
Two thousand seventeen
at six o'clock in the evening
St. Joseph's Catholic Church
Fairview, Pennsylvania

For Jewish ceremonies (approaches will differ by ceremony, and by Orthodox, Conservative, or Reform affiliation):

Mr. and Mrs. Samuel Sherman
and
Mr. and Mrs. Jonas Goldsmith
request the honor of your presence
at the marriage of their children
Abigail
and
Daniel
on Sunday, the fourth of June
Two thousand seventeen
at four o'clock in the afternoon
Congregation Shearith Israel
Two West Seventieth Street
New York

Mr. and Mrs. Samuel Sherman
request the honor of your presence
at the marriage of their daughter
Abigail
to
Mr. Daniel Goldsmith
son of Mr. and Mrs. Jonas Goldsmith

Military Ceremonies

In military weddings, rank determines the placement of names. If the person's rank is lower than sergeant, omit the rank, but list the branch of the service of which he or she is a member:

Mr. and Mrs. Roger Parker
request the honor of your presence
at the marriage of their daughter
Elizabeth Elaine
United States Army
to
Justin James Clark

Junior officer's titles are placed below their names and are followed by their branch of service:

Mr. and Mrs. Roger Parker
request the honor of your presence
at the marriage of their daughter
Elizabeth Elaine
to
Justin James Clark
First Lieutenant, United States Navy

Titles are placed before the names if the rank is higher than lieutenant, and the branch of service is placed on the following line:

Mr. and Mrs. Roger Parker
request the honor of your presence
at the marriage of their daughter
Elizabeth Elaine
to
Captain Justin James Clark
United States Navy

Sample Formal Reception Card

Mr. and Mrs. Roger Parker
request the pleasure of your company
Saturday, the fifth of August
at three o'clock in the afternoon
Fairview Country Club
1638 Eastview Lane
Brookdale, Illinois

Sample Less Formal Reception Card

Reception
immediately following the ceremony
Fairview Country Club
1638 Eastview Lane
Brookdale, Illinois

Sample Response Cards

*M*_____

_____ *accepts*

_____ *regrets*

Saturday, the fifth of August

Fairview Country Club

~~

The favor of your reply is requested
by the fifteenth of July

*M*_____

will attend

The response cards also need envelopes with first-class postage stamps (provided by you). One way to save some money here is to order response postcards—they obviously won't need envelopes, and the cost of postcard stamps is quite a bit less than first-class stamps.

As for those oblivious souls who neglect to return your cards . . . try not to be too hard on them. Make some simple phone calls that tactfully pass over their failures to RSVP, and ask whether they will be attending or not.

Addressing the Envelopes

In this age of technological ease, many brides want to know if it's all right to print envelopes on their computers. Of course you can. It's your wedding, and especially if it's a small and/or informal affair, computer-generated addressing is not going to land you in hot water with the wedding police. However, for traditionally formal affairs, etiquette still dictates writing those envelopes by hand.

INVITATION WORDING WORKSHEET

Wedding invitations:
....
....
....
....
....
....
....
....

Return address for invitation envelopes:
....

Reception cards:
....

Response cards:
....

Return address for response card envelopes:
....

Ceremony cards:
....

Pew cards:
....

Rain cards:
....

Travel cards:
....
....
....
....
....

At-home cards:

....

....

....

....

Return address for at-home card envelopes:

....

....

Thank-you notes:

....

....

Return address for thank-you note envelopes:

....

....

Ceremony programs:

....

....

....

....

....

Party favors:

....

....

Other:

....

....

....

....

Notes:

....

....

....

....

This is a massive undertaking. Give yourself plenty of time, and be realistic. Don't think you're going to write out several hundred envelopes in one sitting.

To address your invitations, you will need the following:

◆ Pens (use black ink only)
◆ Stamps
◆ Invitations, inserts, and envelopes

It's a good idea to ask a few people to help you address your invitations, but don't ask so many that things become chaotic. Make sure the same person who writes the information on the inside of an invitation also addresses its outer envelope. This makes the invitation package look uniform. It also lets the person receiving the invitation know that it was put together with care.

Showing Respect to Certain Professions

Know how to address people of various professions. On the outside envelope, a judge is addressed as The Honorable George Smith. A member of the clergy is most often addressed as The Reverend George Smith or Rabbi George Smith, obviously depending on his religion. A lawyer is addressed as George Smith, Esq. Medical doctors are addressed as Doctor; PhDs are addressed as Dr. Everyone else is Mr., Mrs., or Ms. These are the only abbreviations (aside from Jr.) that are acceptable. Everything else (with the exception of street numbers) is written out.

Inner Envelopes

When addressing the outer envelope, include the full name of the person or persons you are inviting. On the inner envelope, you can be more casual. If you're addressing the outer envelope to Mr. and Mrs. Stephen McGill, feel free to write "Steve and Linda" on the inner envelope, but only if they happen to be your close friends. Otherwise, drop the first name and simply address the inner envelope to Mr. and Mrs. McGill.

One more note on those inner envelopes: remember how careful you had to be when addressing members of various professions on the outer envelope? You're not off the hook yet. While you addressed the judge's outer envelope "The Honorable George Smith," on the inner envelope, he is simply "Judge Smith." The Reverend George Smith is transformed into simply "Reverend Smith," while Rabbi George Smith can be addressed on the inner envelope as "Rabbi Smith."

Specific Addressing Techniques

An Entire Family

If you are inviting the whole family, the parents' names go on the outer envelope, and their children's names are added to the inner envelope descending by age order. (Children's names should come after their parents'.)

> *Mr. and Mrs. Stephen Michael McGill and Family*
> (or *The Smith-McGill Family*)
> *16 Maple Drive*
> *Chestnut Hill, Massachusetts 02555*

On the inner envelope:

> *Mr. and Mrs. McGill*
> *Andrea, Paul, and Meg*

Children who are over eighteen and who are invited to the wedding should receive their own invitations, whether they're living at home or on their own.

An Unmarried Couple Living Together or a Married Couple with Different Last Names

Each person's full name should be on a separate line, with the woman's name listed first.

Outer: Ms. Kathy Smith
    Mr. Neil Jones
Inner: Ms. Smith and Mr. Jones

A Married or Unmarried Same-Sex Couple Using Different Last Names

List the names alphabetically.

Outer: Ms. Nancy Jones
    Ms. Kathy Smith
Inner: Ms. Jones and Ms. Smith

A Married Same-Sex Couple with Hyphenated Last Names

Outer: Mrs. and Mrs. Jennifer and Marie Jones-Smith
Inner: Mrs. and Mrs. Jones-Smith

A Married Same-Sex Couple Using One Last Name

Outer: Mrs. and Mrs. Jennifer and Marie Jones
Inner: Mrs. and Mrs. Jones

And Guest

When you invite a single person with a guest, you're faced with two schools of etiquette: old-school and reality. Old-school etiquette soundly denounces the use of the phrase "and Guest" on the outer envelope of an invitation or on the inner one. In the real world, however, invitations are addressed this way all the time—and just about everyone is fine with it.

Bottom line: if you want to toe the etiquette line on this one, you'll address separate invitations—one to the guest you're inviting, and one to his or her guest. This will require a considerable amount of effort on your part, in that you'll have to track down your guest's guest's address at a time when you're incredibly busy—which is why most brides shun this practice. If you just want to make things easier on yourself (because, after all, isn't it nice of you to allow your friend to invite a guest in the first place?), go ahead and address the outer envelope with the name of your friend or relative. Then add the phrase "and Guest" on the inner envelope following his or her name. Here's a promise: the world will not come to a screeching, horrific end if you choose the latter method.

Other Address Situations

Here are some final points about addressing your invitations.

* Platonic roommates should get their own invitations, even if several of your friends live together. The only instance in which you would send two friends the same invitation is if they are romantically involved or married.
* Although a reply is not expected or required, you should send invitations to everybody involved in the wedding. This includes attendants, siblings, parents, and the officiant, along with their respective significant others.
* You don't need to send invitations to whoever is issuing the invitation.
* Never connect two names with "and" unless the two people are a married couple. If the names are too long to fit on one line, indent the second name under the name on the first line.

Packaging the Invitations

Packing up the invitation and its extras can be as confusing and time-consuming as everything else you've done for your wedding up to this point. What goes where, and why? Here's a method that should make things easier for you:

1. Place the response card face-up under the flap of its envelope (make sure you have already put the postage on the envelopes).
2. Put any extra enclosures (reception cards, maps, directions, and so on) inside the invitation. Put the response card and its envelope inside the invitation as well, on top of the other items. The lettering should be facing upward.
3. Place a small piece of tissue paper over the lettering on the invitation.
4. Place the invitation inside the inner envelope with the lettering facing the back flap. Don't seal this envelope. (The inner envelope is not typically gummed anyway.)
5. Put the inner envelope inside the outer envelope. Again, the writing on the inner envelope should face the flap of the outer envelope.
6. Seal the outer envelope. Make sure the envelope is properly addressed and contains your return address.
7. Stamp and mail the invitations. Instead of wearing out your tongue and the tongues of your friends sealing the envelopes, set up a bowl of clean water and have several thin cloths on hand (like the type you might wipe a counter with). Dip one end of the cloth into the water, wring it out, and wipe the wet end across the gummy portion of the envelope. Take care not to oversaturate the flap, as it may not stick at all, and may also damage the invitation inside.

Before you stamp all those invitations, find out how much postage you will need to mail them. Sometimes, because of heavy paper and lots of inserts, the whole package requires more than a standard first-class stamp. To be on the safe side, take an invitation—one that's completely packaged and ready to go—to the post office and have it weighed. An invitation that's an odd shape (square instead of rectangle, for instance) might also require extra postage and a little extra time. And to really seal the deal on those invitations, ask for love-themed stamps, with images of birds, hearts, rings, or flowers.

Additional Stationery

Depending on the type of wedding you're having, and where, you may need various cards for entrance to the ceremony, special seating, or weather-related contingencies. You'll need some thank-you notes with both your and your new husband's names on them, and you might want to print some formal announcements.

Ceremony Cards

Ceremony cards guaranteeing entrance into the proceedings are not necessary for a traditional wedding site. However, if your wedding is being held at a public place, such as a museum or a historic mansion, you may need some way to distinguish your guests from the tourists (aside from the fact that they will be better dressed than the people hanging out in the snack bar—you hope).

Pew Cards

You will need pew cards (also called "Within the Ribbon" cards) if you wish to reserve seats at the ceremony for any special family members or friends. Have your special guests sit as close as possible to where the action is. Your guests pass the pew cards to the groomsmen at the ceremony, who then know to seat the special guests in the front sections marked off as "Reserved."

Contingency Plans

If there's a chance the ceremony or reception could be upset or moved due to inclement weather, make things easy on yourself. Have cards printed up stating your exact Plan B. While it's everyone's hope that you won't need a backup plan, having cards printed just in case will save you (and your mother, and your bridesmaids) from making possibly hundreds of phone calls should Mother Nature rear an uncooperative head on your wedding day.

Thank-You Notes

You can order thank-you notes that match your invitations, or you can choose something completely different. The note cards can be as formal or informal as you like. If you already have personal stationery, you might consider using that for your thank-you notes instead of ordering something new. It's perfectly proper as far as the rules of etiquette are concerned, and you might save some money.

Announcements

Many couples are not able to invite everyone on their original guest list. Business associates, friends and family members living far away, and others may have been squeezed off the list due to budget or space constraints. Wedding announcements are a convenient way to let people know of your recent nuptials. They are not sent to anyone who received an invitation. (Note: people receiving announcements are under no obligation to buy you a gift.)

Announcements should be mailed immediately after your wedding. You and your fiancé should have them ready before you leave for your honeymoon, and your maid of honor or best man can mail them while you are gone.

INVITATION WORKSHEET

WEDDING INVITATIONS

Description:
....

Manufacturer/Website/Store:
....

Style:
....

Paper:
....

Paper color:
....

Typeface:
....

Ink color:
....

Printing process:
....

Tissue paper inserts:
....

Printed outer envelopes:
....

Inner envelopes:
....

Envelope liner:
....

Number ordered:
....

Cost:

RECEPTION CARDS

Description:
....

Number ordered:
....

Cost:

RESPONSE CARDS

Description:
....

Printed envelopes:
....

Envelope liner:
....

Number ordered:
....

Cost:
....

CEREMONY CARDS

Description:

Number ordered:

Cost:

PEW CARDS

Description:

Number ordered:

Cost:

RAIN CARDS

Description:

Number ordered:

Cost:

TRAVEL CARDS/MAPS

Description:

Number ordered:

Cost:

WEDDING ANNOUNCEMENTS

Description:

Printed envelopes:

Envelope liner:

Number ordered:

Cost:

AT-HOME CARDS

Description:

Printed envelopes:

Envelope liner:

Number ordered:

Cost:

THANK-YOU NOTES

Description:

Printed envelopes:

Envelope liner:

Number ordered:

Cost:

CEREMONY PROGRAMS

Description:

Number ordered:

Cost:

PARTY FAVORS

Description:

Number ordered:

Cost:

OTHER

Description:

Number ordered:

Cost:

Order date:

Ready date: Time:

Delivery/Pick-up instructions:

COST

Total amount due:
....

Amount of deposit: Date:
....

Balance due: Date:
....

Sales tax included?   ◯ Yes   ◯ No
....

Terms of cancellation:
....

....

....

....

....

Notes:
....

....

....

....

....

....

....

....

....

....

....

....

....

....

....

The traditional wording of announcements is as follows:

Mr. and Mrs. Joseph Moran
proudly announce
the marriage of their daughter
Margaret Ann
and
Mr. Justin James McCann
on Saturday, the eighth of July
Two thousand seventeen
Holy Trinity Lutheran Church
Chicago, Illinois

Whoever is named on the invitation as the wedding's host should also be the person or persons announcing the marriage.

When to Order

Order your invitations three to four months before the wedding, and always order more than you need. Don't fool yourself into believing you won't make any mistakes while you're addressing all those envelopes. The last thing you need is a fistfight with your maid of honor because she misspelled a guest's name on the very last one.

Ordering at least twenty extra invitations will lessen the tensions among those writing them out and will also save you the cost of having to place a second order. (The majority of charges for your invitations are for the initial start-up of the press and such; adding a few more to your initial order will cost much less than ordering more later.) Even if you don't make any mistakes, you'll probably want to have a few invitations as keepsakes anyway.

Be sure to leave yourself plenty of time to address and stamp all of those envelopes. If you're planning a wedding near a holiday, mail out your invitations a few weeks earlier to give your guests some extra time to plan. If you plan to invite more guests as regrets come in, send your invitations out at least eight weeks in advance, with a response date of at least three weeks before the wedding.

Pressed for time? Ask your printer to provide you with the envelopes as soon as possible. That way, you can write them while the invitations are being printed.

Do-It-Yourself Projects

Now for some good news. You can print the "extra" stationery projects yourself. These are the things you probably don't spend a huge amount of cash on, but that are really nice for your guests to have. Some great news: if you're talented and have some time to spare, you can even make your own invitations.

Ceremony Programs

Ceremony programs lay out the order of the ceremony, the participants, the music, and the readings. You can add all the personal touches you want. Perhaps you have a favorite poem, quote, or song, which can't be included in the ceremony itself, or maybe there's a special memory you'd like to share, such as how you and your groom met. Programs are easy to print on your computer, and that makes them relatively inexpensive, too. Stationery and online stores have program covers and papers to choose from. The rest is up to you.

Making Your Own Invitations

If you're a particularly gifted artist, or if you're having a less-than-incredibly-formal wedding, you might be thinking about gathering some supplies together and making your own invitations.

If you're up to the challenge and you have the time, there's no reason you shouldn't make your own. Nothing is more interesting than receiving a wedding invitation from a bride or groom who made it lovingly with his or her own hands. A handmade invitation is personalized, obviously. You are, after all, choosing everything that goes on it. You can find instructions for a very easy-to-make invitation in Chapter 6.

Before you decide to do this, recognize your limitations. If you are not artistic in the least (or you have no patience for crafty projects), do not try to make your own wedding invitations. Shower invitations are one thing—they're less formal, there are fewer to construct, and if you make a mistake, you're not as likely to sit and cry over it because of the impending stress of the fast-approaching wedding.

If you decide to create your own invitations, great. Just make sure you have all the supplies you need before you sit down to work, and make a fun weekend out of it. Pop open the wine, offer your helpers some pastries, turn up the music, and start printing and assembling!

CHAPTER 12

Photos and Videos

A PICTURE IS WORTH A THOUSAND WORDS. At no time in your life will this statement seem truer or more appropriate than on your wedding day. You'll be feeling things you can't even recognize, never mind describe—and thanks to the art of photography, you won't have to. A good set of wedding pictures will preserve all the emotions, excitement, and memories for you and your family. Make sure those pictures turn out to be keepers.

Any Photographers Out There?

It's common for the best photographers to be booked a year or more in advance, so start your search early. Begin with the word-of-mouth approach. Ask your friends, family, coworkers, or anyone else you know who has recently coordinated a wedding. Their opinions and wedding shots will go a long way toward helping you find just the right professional for the job.

If you're going on word-of-mouth advice, be sure to ask your friend about her overall experience with the photographer or studio in question. The pictures may be stunning, but the person behind the lens could have been a nightmare—rude, sloppy, and late to the event. If that's the case, keep looking. Your aim is to hire someone who takes great photographs and does so in a way that makes everyone feel at ease. A good photographer is able to relate to you, your groom, and your families, and will bring out the best in everyone.

The Experience Factor

It also goes without saying that you're looking for someone who knows what he is doing. So, how can you grade the photographer's abilities if you don't even know how to work the flash on your own camera? For starters, look for crispness and composition. Did the photographer make good use of lighting, or does the bridal party look washed out and sickly? Were a variety of backgrounds and settings used, or is everyone shown standing in front of the cake? Does he seem to be well versed in the style you're looking for? This should give you an idea of what to look for, but if you have a friend or family member who knows photography, bring her along with you for the interview with the photographer.

When interviewing a photographer who hasn't been recommended to you by a friend or relative (someone you found at a bridal fair or online, for example), ask for references. The photos in the portfolio he's showing you might be incredible, but it's always possible that the person you're talking to bought them from someone else. This philosophy is called "wedding cynicism," and it may save you a lot of headaches down the road. Ask for the names of former clients you can contact to get other customers' points of view.

Asking the Right Questions

Don't be afraid to put your photographer through the wringer a bit. You're probably going to drop a big chunk of change into his pocket if you decide to hire him, so find out before you sign a contract what you're getting into.

- How long has he been in business? Does he specialize in weddings? Is he a full-time photographer?
- What kinds of packages does he offer? What's included in each package? What are the costs for additional photos, flash drives, online hosting, DVDs?
- How many pictures does he typically take at a wedding of your size?
- Is there an hourly fee? Fee for travel?
- Does he use digital equipment, or film, or a combination of both?
- Will you be able to purchase additional pictures in the future?
- Can you see some of his recent work? Can you have the names of some former clients so that you can ask them about their experience with him?

The Digital Revolution Downside

As you'd expect, almost every wedding photographer uses digital technology these days, and this is quite the boon for brides and grooms. Most engaged couples today grew up with digital cameras as the norm, so you probably don't realize that traditional film was much more expensive to work with, gave brides far fewer pictures to choose from, and created a headache when it came time for reprints.

The one downside to the digital age is that it's so easy, some amateur photographers are becoming more and more comfortable marketing themselves as pros, because, as the digital philosophy goes, anyone can shoot digital. Don't fall for this line of thinking. Professional photography—whether the medium is film or pixels—is an art, and it takes more than buying a high-priced digital camera to make someone a master at it.

When you interview a photographer, go ahead and ask how many cameras he carries, what type of lenses he uses, and how many memory cards he typically carries with him. He can probably get great shots with one camera, but he should have at least two lenses: a wide-angle zoom, which is essential for getting shots in tight spaces, and the wide-to-telephoto zoom, which lets the photographer get lots of people in the shot without the weird distortion that can happen with the wide-angle lens. Any lenses he carries on top of these two are, as they say, icing on the cake. And the memory card question is simple: He should have at least two to three in his bag, capable of holding up to 500 shots, although this will depend on how many photos you're signing up for and how confident he is that he can get the shots he needs.

The sage advice here is to steer clear of part-time photographers who only occasionally handle weddings. They're not likely to have the equipment and experience of an expert in the field. You want a full-time photographer, not someone who does this as a hobby, and not someone who's trying to line his pockets by doing this as a side job.

If you really feel the need to give an amateur a whirl, there's more advice for you at the end of this chapter.

Studio Specials

If you're planning on working with a studio, choose one that specializes in weddings. You may love the studio that did your high school graduation picture . . . but if portraits are all they do, they'll probably flunk out at your wedding. Only experienced wedding photographers know all the nuances of photographing a wedding, such as how to deal with problem weather, when to fade into the background, and how to compose a great shot when dealing with a crowd.

If you find a studio you'd like to work with, always ask to see sample wedding photos that were taken by the same photographer who will be working your wedding. If this studio can't or won't supply them, find another studio to work with.

Some studios will charge you a basic hourly rate. Others charge a flat fee for a certain amount of time, such as five consecutive hours of shooting. Studios may also charge for the photographer's travel time, or for overtime if the job runs longer than expected. Like solo photographers, you can expect a studio to lay out different package options for final prints, flash drives, DVDs, and a hosted website where your friends and family can view the wedding pictures in all of their glory. Some studios include albums, frames, and special parents' books as part of the deal.

Ask for the prices up-front. And ask for a price list for additional photos, as you may want to order more at a later date.

Picture Perfect

After you've chosen the photographer, sit down with him and discuss your wants, needs, and expectations. It's important to establish a good relationship well before the wedding so that everyone feels comfortable when the big, frenzied day arrives.

There are, of course, the traditional wedding poses and shots, which will almost surely be included in your package. If you have anything else in mind, let your photographer know, ASAP! Give him a list of all of the special people you want included in the pictures, especially anyone who isn't in the wedding party.

Choose a Style

The photojournalistic style is probably the most popular option right now for wedding pictures. These are the photos that appear to be taken when no one's paying attention, and they can produce some unforgettable images. Emotions are captured in a more natural state. Frozen smiles and uncomfortable poses are nowhere to be seen. Tight shots blend with wide scenes to truly tell the entire story of the day. Many couples do a hybrid of traditional, posed shots with photojournalistic pictures. If you're interested in this style, however, be sure to ask your photographer if he has done these shots in the past and ask to see samples. This is a very specific style of photography, and it can't be attempted for the first time on your wedding day.

Formal Photos Before the Wedding

Although it's considered bad luck for the groom to see the bride before the ceremony, many couples feel comfortable doing away with this superstition and taking the formal shots before the wedding. This makes life easier for a lot of people. The photographer doesn't have to rush to get all the shots on your list before hungry guests start a riot, the guests don't suffer from starvation or boredom while they wait for you to pose . . . pose . . . and pose again, and you get to enjoy more of the reception.

If seeing the groom before the ceremony is absolutely out of the question for you, try to take as many of the formal pictures as you can without him—you alone, you and your parents, you and your attendants, and so on. At the reception, speed things up by making sure everyone who's going to be in a picture knows where he or she is supposed to be. You can also look for ways to be together without seeing each other—blindfolded, for example, in your wedding garb, or standing on opposite sides of an open door.

Shooting on Location

Some couples opt to take their formal wedding photos at a location other than the reception site. Sometimes the spot they select is of great sentimental value; sometimes it's chosen just because the scenery is gorgeous. Some popular photo-shoot locations include a beach, a lake, or a garden (in the spring and summer), near foliage (in the fall), and snow-covered woods (in the winter).

If you do plan to take your photo shoot on the road, remember that your guests will have to wait even longer than usual to see you (and their dinner) at the reception. As a way to ease their impatience (and their stomachs), make sure that the reception site will be offering bar service and hors d'oeuvres while they wait for you to arrive.

Black and White

Though you may associate black-and-white photos with your parents' and grandparents' weddings, they can also add a special touch to yours. Color may be brilliant, but black and white creates atmosphere and style, and gives your photos a timeless feel that's perfect for an occasion like this. Your photographer can shoot in color and convert chosen images to black and white later. This is a simple process, and it shouldn't cost you a thing.

Photographic Extras

Aside from working with you on the wedding day, you may want the photographer to take an engagement photo and/or a formal bridal portrait. If so, you'll need to iron out the details with the photographer in your initial meeting. Some brides have portraits taken as a gift to their parents. Photos can also be used as part of a wedding announcement in the newspaper.

PHOTOGRAPHER WORKSHEET

Name of photographer/studio:
....

Address:
....

Website:
....

Telephone:
....

Contact:
....

Hours they can be reached:
....

Directions:
....

APPOINTMENTS

Date: Time:
....

Date: Time:
....

Date: Time:
....

Name of package *(if applicable)*:   # of pictures:
....

Date of hired services: Time:
....

Number of hours: Overtime cost:
....

Travel fee:
....

Fee for website:
....

Fee for custom pages:
....

Fee per flash drive:
....

Fee for album inscription:
....

Additional fees *(if any)*:
....

Engagement session included? ◯ Yes ◯ No   Additional cost, if any:
....

Will attend rehearsal? ◯ Yes ◯ No   Additional cost, if any:
....

Additional cost, if any:
....

Type of wedding album included:
....

Date photos will be available for viewing:
....

....

Additional services included:
....

....

....

....

....

....

COST

Total amount due:
....

Amount of deposit: Date:
....

Balance due: Date:
....

Sales tax included? ○ Yes ○ No
....

Terms of cancellation:
....

....

Notes:
....

....

....

....

....

....

....

....

....

PHOTOGRAPH CHECKLIST WORKSHEET

INCLUDED IN PACKAGE

Item	Number Included in Package	Cost of Each Additional	Notes
8" × 10" engagement portraits			
5" × 7" engagement prints			
4" × 5" engagement prints			
Wallet size engagement prints			
Wedding proofs			
Wallet size prints			
3½" × 5" prints			
4" × 5" prints			
5" × 7" prints			
8" × 10" prints			
11" × 14" portraits			
Other prints *(list below)*			
Preview album			
Wedding album			
Wedding album pages			
Parent albums			
Other *(list below)*			

PHOTOGRAPH CHECKLIST WORKSHEET (CONTINUED)

Give a copy of this completed form to your wedding photographer.

Name of bride and groom:
....

Address:
....

....

Telephone:
....

Wedding date:
....

Ceremony location:
....

Reception location:
....

Special instructions:
....

....

PORTRAITS

❍ You and the groom during the ceremony *(if possible)*
....

❍ An official wedding portrait of you and your groom
....

❍ The entire wedding party
....

❍ You, your groom, and family members
....

❍ You and your mother
....

❍ You and your father
....

❍ You with both parents
....

❍ You with your groom's parents *(your new in-laws)*
....

❍ The groom with his mother
....

❍ The groom with his father
....

○ The groom with both parents

○ The groom with your parents *(his new in-laws)*

○ Combination photos of the attendants

○ You and your groom with any special people in your lives, such as grandparents or godparents

○ Other:

PHOTOS FROM THE CEREMONY (IF POSSIBLE)

○ Each member of the wedding party as he or she comes down the aisle

○ The mother of the bride as she is ushered down the aisle

○ The groom's parents

○ You and your father coming down the aisle

○ Your father leaving you at the altar

○ The wedding party at the altar

○ The ring exchange

○ The vows

○ The lighting of any candles or special ceremony features

○ Any relatives or friends who participate in the ceremony by doing a reading or lighting a candle

○ The kiss

○ The walk from the altar

○ Other:

....

....

....

CANDID

○ Getting ready for the ceremony; putting on the veil, the garter
....

○ The bridesmaids, and you with them before the wedding
....

○ You and your father leaving
....

○ You and your father arriving at the ceremony
....

○ Getting out of the limousine/car
....

○ You and your groom getting in the car
....

○ Toasting one another in the car
....

○ Reception arrival
....

○ The first dance
....

○ The cutting of the cake
....

○ Tossing the bouquet
....

○ Removing/tossing the garter
....

○ Going-away dance
....

○ Leaving for the honeymoon *(possibly with a "just married" sign on the car)*
....

○ Other:
....

....

....

Bridal portraits are usually taken either at the photographer's studio or at the bridal salon on the day of your last fitting. Most photographers will meet you at the salon, but you should double-check to make sure.

If your photography budget is overflowing with extra funds, you might consider thank-you notes that feature a picture of you and your groom. You can get one standard photo that goes on every note, or, if you're really ambitious, personalize each thank-you note with a photo of you opening the person's gift.

Videography

The bride and groom are, ironically, the two people who usually remember the least about their wedding. They're in a fog of emotion and excitement, in which hundreds of sensory impressions go by in a blur. Still photographs will show you a few staged poses, but video will show how things were. You can have a record of the guests as they sing, dance, eat, kiss, cry, and laugh. When a bride and groom finally sit down to watch their wedding video, it will certainly bring back memories, but it will also show them many things that they were not able to notice during the wedding.

Your Videographer

Don't leave the videography to a friend or relative unless you've seen a sample of her work and *were impressed by it*. When searching for a videographer, apply the same basic guidelines you would for a still photographer. The pictures may be moving, but the images should still be crisp and clear, and colors should be true to life.

Confirm that your videographer has up-to-date, quality equipment, and not a forty-year-old eight-millimeter camera. Also, ask about editing and dubbing, microphones (will you both be wearing one during the ceremony, for instance, or will only the groom be wired for sound?), and lights. Find out how many cameras he has, and how many people will be assisting on the job. Some video formats require the simultaneous use of two cameras; one person with one camera will bring you up short.

Ask to view samples. You're looking for smooth editing, clear sound, and an overall professional look and feel to the video. With all the technology available today, you don't have to settle for anything short of broadcast-quality production values. Once you've found someone and verified references, get a written contract stipulating costs, services, operators, and of course, the date, time, and place.

Interviewing Candidates

Again, you'll be putting on your bold bridal cap and asking a total stranger questions. Remember that it's in your best interest to ask as many questions as you feel pertinent to the candidate at hand. The previous section covered information about the videographer's equipment. Here are some other things to ask:

- How long has he been doing this professionally?
- Can you see some of his most recent work? Is he working on a video that you can see? (Again, this is the wedding cynicism philosophy—you want to make sure this person has actually done the work that you're looking at.)
- What kinds of packages does he offer? What are the rates? Are there any other fees, such as travel, hourly, and so on?
- Does he use any special effects in the final product, such as subtitles, credits, music, and so on?
- Ask for the names of former clients so that you can talk to them about their experiences with him.

When you're viewing samples of the videographer's work, consider whether the segments tell a story. In other words, does the video make sense to you? Is everything in chronological order? Are the "big events," like the ceremony and the cake-cutting, shown clearly? How's the sound? Is the editing smooth? Is the picture steady and focused?

There are some very elaborate video formats out there, some featuring special lenses and special effects. Before you get carried away with the idea of seeing your name in lights, remember that little technicality called a budget. Like the photo package, the typical wedding video package costs anywhere from several hundred to several thousand dollars, depending on the quality of the equipment, the number of hours you've contracted the videographer for, the number of cameras, the amount of editing, and other factors. Remember to determine what's most important to you, figure out what you can afford, and go from there.

Friends As Photographers

It's really tempting to offer a friend a couple of hundred dollars to take your digital wedding photos. After all, you have a camera, you know how easy it is to use—what could go wrong?

Well, there are a couple of things to keep in mind when you're considering making this leap of faith. First, getting all of the shots that you want and expect is a bigger job than it may seem. It requires a lot of organization of thoughts, schedules, and (most difficult of all) people. A professional has dealt with this reality many, many times, and knows just how to wrangle everyone and everything to give you exactly what you want.

Second, you're more likely to get homey snapshots (as opposed to amazing, frame-worthy photographs) of your wedding when using a friend. "Innovative" angles could turn into a mess, and bad lighting could turn your time in the spotlight into the stuff of

VIDEOGRAPHER WORKSHEET

Name of videographer/studio:
....

Address:
....

Website:
....

Telephone:
....

Contact:
....

Hours they can be reached:
....

Directions:
....

APPOINTMENTS

Date: .... Time: ....

Date: .... Time: ....

Date: .... Time: ....

Name of package *(if applicable)*:
....

Date of hired services: .... Time: ....

Number of hours:
....

Number of cameras:
....

Overtime cost:
....

Travel fee:
....

Additional fees *(if any)*:
....

Will attend rehearsal? ◯ Yes ◯ No   Additional cost, if any:
....

Length of video:
....

Date video will be ready:

DVD WILL INCLUDE

Prewedding preparations: ◯ Yes ◯ No
....

Notes:
....

....

Individual interviews with bride and groom prior to ceremony: ⭘ Yes ⭘ No

Notes:

Ceremony: ⭘ Yes ⭘ No   Notes:

Reception: ⭘ Yes ⭘ No   Notes:

Photomontage: ⭘ Yes ⭘ No   Notes:

Other:

PACKAGE INCLUDES

Sound: ⭘ Yes ⭘ No   Notes:

Music: ⭘ Yes ⭘ No   Notes:

Unedited version of wedding events: ⭘ Yes ⭘ No   Notes:

Edited version of wedding events: ⭘ Yes ⭘ No   Notes:

Price of additional copies:

Other:

ADDITIONAL SERVICES INCLUDED

Cost:

Total amount due:

Amount of deposit: Date:

Balance due: Date:

Sales tax included? ⭘ Yes ⭘ No

Terms of cancellation:

Notes:

wedding album nightmares. But if you're willing to take the risk, you could end up with a boatload of fun pictures for a minimum cost. Just don't expect your non-pro pal to rig a ladder to get an overview of the dance floor, or to successfully color-correct an underexposed photo after the fact.

Other Issues

In addition to artistic troubles, your photographer/friend may not be prepared to spend your entire wedding working, particularly if she would have attended as a normal guest otherwise, or if she knows a large number of your attendees. Since you probably wouldn't have a formal agreement or contract with her, you have no guarantee that she won't spend the majority of the occasion behaving like any normal guest: eating, drinking, dancing, and schmoozing with friends, stopping to take a picture every now and then. Wedding photographers have to be on the ball at all times; one brief chitchat could result in them missing the father-daughter dance or cake-cutting.

Essentially, it's important for you to know that if you informally ask a friend to take pictures—or perform in any vendor capacity, for that matter—without a written, signed agreement, you have no legal recourse for a job poorly done. If you use a professional photographer, he will provide a formal, written agreement that legally protects both of you—if your pictures do not come back at a high quality or things that you were promised are not delivered, you can refer to the agreement and at the very least, get some of your money back.

With a friend, unless you draw up a written agreement (which could be messy in and of itself), you are left unprotected, and in the worst-case scenario, without pictures of the most important day of your life. However, if you have the utmost faith in your friend and you don't mind that your pictures may not be wedding-magazine quality, this option could work for you.

CHAPTER 13

Ceremony and Reception Music

HAVE YOU EVER BEEN TO A WEDDING where the music was so bad you wished there hadn't been any? You certainly don't want anyone to remember your wedding this way, so you'll have to put some careful thought into the musical aspects of your big day. Remember that the right music adds emotion and drama to the occasion; the wrong music kills anything you've got going. Take your time in choosing not only the perfect music but also the perfect musicians.

Coming and Going

Carefully selected music can provide atmosphere and enhance the mood and meaning of your ceremony. You may already have an auditory fantasy of the music that will be playing as you walk down the aisle, as you take your vows, and as you leave the church. This section offers suggestions for your ceremony music—but remember that they are only suggestions. If, for example, you'd like a slow, somber (read: dramatic) piece to play while you walk down the aisle instead of a chirpy little tune, go for it. It's your wedding day; choose the music that will make it feel right to you. Also, if you are planning on having a church ceremony, bear in mind that some churches have restrictions on which music is and is not allowed, so be sure to check with your officiant before you get your heart set on walking down the aisle to one particular tune!

The Processional

The processional is the music that accompanies the wedding party in their jaunt down the aisle. A traditional march helps to set the pace for some nervous feet—but a lighter, airy piece might lift your heart as you take those first steps toward your soon-to-be-husband.

When it's time for you to make that long trek down the aisle, you can walk to the same piece that you've chosen for the bridesmaids or to your own music. Sometimes the piece is the same but played at a different tempo, or with an audience-captivating pause before it begins. Brides differ widely in their preferences for their processional pieces. Here are some timeless suggestions:

- Wagner's "Bridal Chorus" ("Here comes the bride . . .") from the opera *Lohengrin*
- Mendelssohn's "Wedding March" from *A Midsummer Night's Dream* suite

- Bach's "Sheep May Safely Graze"
- Stanley's "Trumpet Voluntary"
- Pachelbel's Canon in D
- Handel's "Hornpipe" from *Water Music* suite
- Charpentier's "Prelude" from *Te Deum*

Wagner's "Bridal Chorus" is the processional that many people think of when they picture a bride marching down the aisle; its bookend is Mendelssohn's slightly more upbeat "Wedding March," which is often used as recessional music.

The Recessional

The big exit! The song should be joyous and upbeat, reflecting your happiness at being joined for life to the man now accompanying you down the aisle and out of the church. An upbeat song will also help move your guests along out of the church more quickly than a sedate piece. In addition, if the reception is following the ceremony, the guests will be happy for an excuse to bound (rather than stroll) out of the church.

Take another look at the titles listed in the section on the processional. Many of these pieces can be used at either the beginning or the end of the ceremony. Some other classic suggestions include:

- Widor's "Toccata" from Symphony for Organ No. 5
- Purcell's "Trumpet Tune"
- Willan's "Finale Jubilante" from *Five Pieces*
- Handel's "Sinfonia (Arrival of the Queen of Sheba)" from the oratorio *Solomon*
- Vierne's "Finale" from Organ Symphony No. 1
- Wesley's "Choral Song"

Ceremony Soundtrack

If additional musicians, singers, and songs are an option you'd like to consider, consult with the officiant. As mentioned before, some religions place restrictions on secular musical selections during the ceremony, but other religions may be very flexible. Ask about your music well in advance of the big day so that there are no surprises or misunderstandings the day before or, worse, the day of the ceremony.

Note that most songs listed in this section are of the classical (in other words, more likely to be approved by a minister) variety. If you have the latitude to choose popular music, then two rules apply:

- Remember that even the most secular ceremony is celebrating a sacred union between you and your groom. Scan lyrics thoroughly to make sure they are appropriate for the occasion.
- Keep your guests in mind. This may entail walking a fine line between the music you want for your wedding ceremony and what the people who have traveled 500 miles to share the day with you will deem appropriate. Think of this as a sub-bullet of Rule 1 here: If the lyrics to a given song are going to offend your grandmother, think twice about including it in your ceremony.

The Prelude

The prelude lasts from the time the guests start arriving until all of them are seated and the mother of the bride (traditionally the last-seated guest before the wedding party comes down the aisle) is ready to make her entrance. The options for music here are very broad: upbeat, slow, or a mixture of both. The prelude establishes a mood and entertains the guests while they wait. The end of the prelude, right before the processional, is usually a good time for a soloist or choir to break into song. During the final piece of the prelude, the mother of the bride is seated. Some good classical choices for the prelude include:

+ Handel's *Water Music*
+ Mozart's "Adagio" from *Ave Verum*
+ Vivaldi's "Largo" from "Winter" (*The Four Seasons*)
+ Bach's *Brandenburg Concertos*
+ Bach's "Jesu, Joy of Man's Desiring"
+ Bach's Eight Short Preludes and Fugues for the Organ
+ Mendelssohn's "Adagio" from Organ Sonata No. 2
+ Peeters's "Aria" from Sonata for Trumpet and Piano
+ Massenet's "Meditation" from the opera *Thais*

Ceremony Music

The right music played during the actual wedding ceremony can enhance the mood and emphasize the meaning of the service. Consider playing a short piece during the lighting of the unity candle, for example. If Communion is being incorporated as part of the ceremony, this is a good time for a vocal performance.

If you're getting married in a church, chances are your musical choices will be limited to religious songs. Paul Stookey's "The Wedding Song" is a golden-oldie hit that just may make the cut in your house of worship. Some other, non-Top-40 songs to consider are:

+ Schubert's "Ave Maria"
+ Artman's "Wedding Prayer"
+ Malotte's "The Lord's Prayer"
+ Wetherill's "A Marriage Prayer"
+ Traditional, "The Irish Wedding Song"
+ Franck's "Panis Angelicus"

- Callahan's "Wherever You Go"
- Dvořák's "God Is My Shepherd"
- Peeters's "Wedding Song: Whither Thou Goest, There Will I Go Also"

Now, whether your church organist and/or soloist knows any of these songs is another matter altogether. Be sure to meet with your musicians to discuss your choices before the ceremony.

Finding Your Church Musicians

Before you hire a full orchestra to accompany the church choir, remember that the cost of musicians and singers for the ceremony must fit into your overall music budget. In other words, don't hire a string quartet for $1,000 if you have only $1,200 allotted for ceremony *and* reception music. It may take some fancy footwork, but don't be intimidated. You can have wonderful music for both events with a little compromise and ingenuity.

If you regularly attend a church that employs an awful organist and/or singer, he or she is the last one you want commandeering the music for your ceremony. Most churches will allow you to bring in your own musicians, provided they meet the church's guidelines. In other words, unless you belong to a very progressive church, your favorite local hard-rock band probably won't be allowed to set up in the choir loft.

If your friends are no help and your church doesn't have a wedding coordinator, you'll have to hit the wedding-music circuit in town. Sit through some weddings—if you hear a great soloist, grab him or her after the ceremony and make arrangements to meet and discuss your wedding. The great thing about attending other weddings is that you'll be exposed to all sorts of other musicians (string quartets, trumpet players) and you'll get a million musical ideas for your own big day.

Still at a loss? Ask the music department at your local high school or college if there are any particularly gifted students who sing (or play the trumpet, piano, violin) at weddings. Seek out the director of the music program at a local college. Look in the classified section of your newspaper. Musicians for hire are out there and they want the work; you just have to find them.

Rockin' the Reception

These days, the big decision about music is whether to hire a band or a DJ. When it comes to price, the DJ is definitely the less expensive option, but there are other factors that may influence your choice. Whichever you choose, you will want to finalize arrangements approximately six months in advance of your wedding date.

Live Bands

If you're lucky enough to find live musicians who can work with your budget, book them quickly—before another bride hires your band for her wedding. If you're not so lucky, plan to make many treks to bars, lounges, and function halls—any place where you might find some decent live music. When you find a group that strikes your fancy, go back and listen to them again. Some bands will impress you the first time—but you have no idea whether they're having an especially good (or lucky) night, or whether they always sound like they should be playing arenas.

In addition to the band's sound, look for a variety of musical styles and tempos in their repertoire. Do they play seven slow songs, one fast number, then two more slow ones, or do they know how to vary the pace? Do they appear to be enjoying themselves, or do they look like they'd rather be somewhere else?

Once you find a band you like, make arrangements with the leader to sit down and talk about exactly what you want concerning

CEREMONY MUSIC WORKSHEET

Organist's name:
....

Address: .... Telephone: ....

Fee:
....

Soloist's name:
....

Address: .... Telephone: ....

Fee:
....

Name of other musician, if applicable:
....

Address: .... Telephone: ....

Fee:
....

....

....

Part of Ceremony	Musical Selection	Performed By
Prelude:		
Processional:		
During the ceremony:		
(list specific part below)		
Recessional:		
Other:		

your wedding. Have a list of songs ready that they have to play at your reception. If they don't know the songs already, will they attempt to learn them in time? Ask about their sound system and equipment needs. If your reception site is too small, or doesn't have the proper electrical outlets and fuse power, it's better to know before you hire the band.

Before you sign a contract with the band, make sure the following commitments are stipulated in writing:

+ **The band's attire.** You don't want them showing up at a formal wedding in ripped jeans or wrinkled khakis.
+ **The band's arrival time.** Make sure the band is set up, with instruments tuned, before the guests arrive at the reception. The band's sound check will not make for soothing dinner music.
+ **The exact cost of hiring the band . . . and everything included in that price.** Some bands charge you if they have to add an extra piece of equipment; others charge a fee for playing requests; and others charge for travel. And take note: you have to feed them, so add them to your final head count for dinner.

This is also the time to make sure the band knows the exact location of the reception. There have actually been instances where the musical talent has shown up at the reception site with the right name, but in the wrong city.

DJ Wedding Is in the House

DJs can obviously provide more variety than bands and give you the original version of songs, and they don't cause as many logistical headaches. DJs are seen as slightly less formal than bands, but they're also considerably less expensive, which adds a great deal to their appeal.

It's just as important to see and hear a DJ in action as it is with a band. Look for the same things you would in a band: balance, variety, a good mix of fast and slow songs, a good personality, and first-rate equipment. Could this person perform the duties of master of ceremonies? Does he talk way too much or far too little? Does he spend an inordinate amount of time marketing his wares during the reception?

Find out how big his music collection is, because your disc jockey should be able to accommodate the majority of your guests' requests. Provide a list of what you want played at the reception, and if you have some songs you absolutely, positively, upon penalty of death do *not* want played, give him a (short) list of those, too! However, be prepared to compromise and trust the DJ's musical judgment. His main interest is playing music that will jump-start your party. Some other questions to ask your DJ include the following:

◆ How many weddings has he provided music for? What size weddings does he typically work?
◆ Will he provide appropriate music for the cocktail hour?
◆ Can he provide a wireless microphone for any toasts or speeches?
◆ Is the gratuity included in the price?

The DJ's exact cost, including possible extras, the time of arrival and departure, the place, and his proper attire should all be spelled out in the contract. It is also possible that your DJ will have to sign another agreement with your reception site; these agreements typically involve what time the DJ is permitted to enter the facility and set up, noise control, speaker wattage, and what kinds of equipment he is permitted to use. For example, some venues do not mind flashing lights, but do not allow bubble or dry ice machines.

DIY DJ?

With the advent of MP3 files and laptops allowing practically anyone to become a DJ, even less-than-technically-savvy couples want to know why they should pay someone to pick the tunes for the most special day of their lives. And the answer is . . . if you're brave and willing to put the time into truly crafting (not just creating) a playlist for your wedding, you can do it yourself. But there are some commitment issues to contend with:

♦ You have to be willing to choose a variety of music. Yes, you love your obscure music and affectionately refer to yourself as a music snob. If you didn't read it earlier in this chapter, read it now: A DJ's (even a DIY DJ's) job is to get people up on the dance floor and keep them there. And people tend to gravitate toward music they know. So go ahead and throw a couple of obscure tunes in there if people will dance to them, but keep most of the music dance-friendly.

♦ A DJ will definitely give more attention to the young folks, who are most likely to get up and shake their groove on the dance floor, but he knows that your elders would like to do a little dancing, too.

♦ Invest in volume. Reception music needs to be loud enough to fill the space, but not so loud as to deafen the crowd. In other words, your laptop speakers are not going to do the trick for your reception. You'll need to purchase or rent appropriate sound equipment to send your playlist soaring, but keep in mind that this is not a concert. People seated at tables will want to be able to talk over the music.

♦ Master the cross-fade. You'll note that a DJ abhors silence. The end of one song fades out over the beginning of another. It's called the cross-fade, and it's a technique you have to master in your own wedding playlist.

◆ Don't leave creating the playlist for the last minute. It's a time-consuming (but fun) project. Consider the tempo of the songs you're choosing, and when to throw in a slow number or two (at the very most). Once the playlist is solidified, do not let anyone (except a professional DJ) tinker with it. Unfortunately, when your playlist arrives on a laptop, some guests may think they have free rein to mix it up. Appoint your largest groomsman or most assertive bridesmaid (or vice versa) as keeper of the music during the reception.

The Songs

No matter what kind of musical talent you decide on in the end, you'll need to have an idea of the music you want played during the reception. If you're following tradition and including the first dance with your groom, and then a dance with your dad, and the groom's dance with his mother, you'll have to tell your bandleader or DJ which songs you want to hear at those moments.

Your choices for reception music are limited only by your imagination. The only guideline you should be aware of is that you want to *entertain* your guests—not drive them away. It's an added bonus if the music complements the theme and style of the day. In other words, for a very formal wedding, a swing ensemble or jazz quartet might go over a bit better than an alternative-music band. Whatever type(s) of music you choose, remember that this entertainment is a little gift to your guests to add to their enjoyment of your wedding. Your best bet is to go with an all-inclusive song list that covers a broad spectrum of musical tastes—slow, dance tunes, rock, and soul.

RECEPTION MUSIC WORKSHEET

Name of band/DJ:
....

Address:
....

Website:
....

Telephone:
....

Manager/Contact:
....

Hours he or she can be reached:
....

Number of performers:
....

Description of act:
....

....

Demo available?   ◯ Yes ◯ No
....

Notes:
....

View live performance?   ◯ Yes ◯ No
....

Date: Time: Location:
....

....

Appointments:
....

Date: Time:
....

Date: Time:
....

Date: Time:
....

....

Date of hired services: Time:
....

Number of hours:
....

Cocktail hour:
....

Overtime cost:
....

Includes the following services:
....

....

....

Equipment provided:

....

....

....

....

Equipment rented:

....

....

....

....

Rental costs:

....

....

....

....

Cost:

Total amount due:

Amount of deposit: Date:

Balance due: Date:

Terms of cancellation:

....

....

Notes:

....

....

....

....

CHAPTER 14

Flowers and Floral Design

TO MANY PEOPLE, flowers are the ultimate symbol of love. The beauty, the fragrance, the romance—everything about flowers, it seems, has captivated the imagination throughout history. Flowers are such an important part of the wedding décor that some might say they make or break the scene. The wrong flowers say, "Ho-hum," while the right ones shout, "Look at ME!"

Your Flower Budget

Before you get swept away by all the beauty and romance of flowers, you must calculate your flower budget. Flowers are one of those wedding expenses that can get out of hand quickly. The tab for this expense tends to add up in a hurry, even when you're trying to keep things under control. But if you're careful (and maybe a little crafty), you can bring your pretty posies in under budget—without sacrificing anything in the way of atmosphere.

Get Creative

Whether you decide to work with a florist or to do your wedding flowers yourself, you don't have to stick to the same old thing you've seen at every other wedding you've been to. But there's something to be said for following some of the old traditions, such as carrying a bouquet or decorating the altar in church with many arrangements. Assuming you're working with an adequate budget, there's nothing stopping you from taking your floral fantasies to the absolute limit. This section contains some ideas for getting imaginative with your wedding décor.

Centerpieces

Many brides choose *not* to include flowers in the centerpieces at the reception, which is one way to save, using the technical term, *a ton* of money. A crystal or glass bowl with floating candles is a lovely option—and if you place the bowls on mirrors, you can illuminate the room with streaks of light.

Instead of going with a traditional arrangement, one trend you'll see nowadays is placing flowers in several small silver vases and grouping them together as one centerpiece. Then you can invite your guests to take the vases home. You might also want to take small candies—conversation hearts, candied almonds, even rose petals—and sprinkle them around the centerpieces. Discuss and confirm all reception centerpiece ideas with the venue site before going on a shopping spree at the craft store; for example, many venues no longer allow open-flame candles without a hurricane glass covering up at least to the top of the flame.

Cover It!

If you're a bride who just can't have enough floral and greenery and tulle at your wedding, take a good look at your ceremony and reception site. Does either have any pillars? Banisters? Railings? Pews? If so, start swagging! You can add garlands, ivy, and/or tulle to any of these structures and really bring them to life. (You can find garlands of faux greenery in any craft shop, and tulle is relatively inexpensive.) This is also a great idea if you're getting married outdoors in a pavilion or gazebo and need to dress it up a bit.

If your reception site is looking a little bare, think about placing some potted trees near the entrance. Or maybe you'd prefer a balloon arrangement. Consider using a combination of gold, clear, ivory, or white balloons as the main colors and then add a few balloons that match your bridesmaids' dresses. You can also buy colored confetti to put inside the clear balloons.

Be sure that your sites permit outside decorations and will allow you extra time to set them up and take them down. You also might have to put someone in charge of taking the decorations home afterward, especially if you want to keep them. Unless stated otherwise, the reception site has no responsibility to store your supplies; they may throw them out after your celebration, or even charge you for leaving them behind.

Twinkle, Twinkle

So you've draped everything you could get your hands on with ivy, flowers, and tulle, and it still isn't enough. How about adding some little white lights to the mix? They're pretty, they're understated, and they give everyone the feeling that they're looking at a starry sky. If you're adding potted trees to your reception site, these lights are a particularly easy way to dress them up a bit. As an added safety measure, check out solar twinkle lights—they don't need electricity; they soak up energy from natural light and glow!

Finding the Florist

An honest florist, when presented with a set-in-stone budget, will steer you in the most practical direction. Good florists know there's nothing to be gained by showing you things you can't afford. But if you don't have the slightest idea what your flower budget is, then you can't really fault a florist for showing you her most expensive arrangements. Once the budget has been settled, you can concentrate on choosing the flowers you can actually use.

If you have trouble getting florist referrals from friends, ask your reception site coordinator, visit online review hubs, or visit florists' booths at wedding exhibitions. Ask for photos of previous displays that the florist has created, and check references to make sure that she has a history of quality work for actual customers.

Once you pick a florist, you'll need a written contract stipulating costs, times, dates, places, and services. Make sure the florist is scheduled to arrive *before* the photographer on your wedding day, so you won't end up with a wedding album filled with you, your bridesmaids . . . and an eerie lack of nosegays.

FLORIST WORKSHEET

Name of florist:
....

Address:
....

Website:
....

Telephone: Contact:
....

Hours:
....

Directions:
....

APPOINTMENTS

Date: Time:
....

Date: Time:
....

Date: Time:
....

Services provided:
....

....

Date of delivery: Time:
....

Location of bridal party:
....

Travel fee:
....

Additional fees *(if any)*:
....

COST

Total amount due:
....

Amount of deposit: Date:
....

Balance due: Date:
....

Sales tax included? ◯ Yes ◯ No
....

Terms of cancellation:
....

....

Notes:
....

When Your Florist Talks . . .

Before you meet with your florist, decide on a color scheme for your wedding. Bring color swatches (of bridesmaids' dresses and/or decorations) along to your meeting with the florist so she can recommend flowers that will either match or complement the overall scheme.

Your florist will also guide you to the flowers that most suit your style, taste, and even your skin tone. If you're very petite, for instance, the florist will probably advise that you not carry a huge, elaborate arrangement because it will overwhelm you. If you're particularly fair-skinned, you might be advised against an all-white bouquet, because the lack of color in your flowers will only emphasize the lack of color in your cheeks.

She will also tell you which flowers will look best in the ceremony and reception locations you've chosen. If you're getting married in a huge cathedral, for example, you'll need more substantial pieces than if you're saying your vows in a teeny tiny chapel. If the florist has never done work at either site before, take a trip there together so you can both look around and discuss what will be needed—and where.

Delivery

When hammering out the final details with your florist, make sure you're both clear on the delivery schedule. If you plan to take pictures two hours before the ceremony, chances are you want to be photographed holding your flowers, not standing there empty-handed. Communication is vital. Make sure you can have your flowers where and when you want them.

Flowers for Your Honored Guests

What about flowers for guests of honor? Along with that bouquet you will (or won't) be tossing, you'll have to choose arrangements for the wedding party, your mother, your groom's mother, and for any grandmothers.

The Bridesmaids

In most weddings, the bridesmaids carry their flowers rather than wear them. These arrangements can range from elaborate bouquets to simple groupings—or even a single long-stemmed rose. (You may decide to add something special to the maid of honor's flowers as a way of making her stand out in the crowd.)

Floral hairpieces can be a lovely touch for your bridesmaids. Be sure to discuss hairstyles with your bridesmaids and your florist. It would be very frustrating to spend money for flowers that won't stay in your maid of honor's hair because she's decided to wear it loose, or because her hair is too short.

If you're having a flower girl, she'll need a basket of flowers or petals or a small bouquet. Again, be sure the florist has a good idea of what the flower girl will be wearing so that she chooses appropriate flowers.

Who Else?

The mothers of the marrying couple usually receive special corsages just before the ceremony begins. You might also want to include flowers for anyone who's playing a special role in the ceremony, such as your readers, the gift bearers, and so on. You won't forget wedding flowers for the mothers and grandmothers (you hope), but make sure you also remember to include any great-grandmothers and godmothers.

WEDDING PARTY FLOWERS WORKSHEET

Person/Item	Description	Number	Cost
BRIDE			
Bouquet			
Headpiece			
Toss-away bouquet			
Going-away corsage			
MAID/MATRON OF HONOR			
Bouquet			
Headpiece			
BRIDESMAIDS			
Bouquet			
Headpiece			
FLOWER GIRLS			
Flowers			
Basket			
Headpiece			
MOTHERS OF THE BRIDE AND GROOM			
Corsage			
GRANDMOTHERS OF THE BRIDE AND GROOM			
Corsage			

WEDDING PARTY FLOWERS WORKSHEET (CONTINUED)

Person/Item	Description	Number	Cost
GROOM			
Boutonniere			
BEST MAN			
Boutonniere			
USHERS			
Boutonniere			
RINGBEARER			
Boutonniere			
Pillow			
FATHERS OF THE BRIDE AND GROOM			
Boutonniere			
GRANDFATHERS OF THE BRIDE AND GROOM			
Boutonniere			
READERS			
Corsage			
Boutonniere			
OTHER (LIST BELOW)			
TOTAL			

Flowers for the men are pretty simple. The groomsmen wear boutonnieres. Sometimes the boutonniere is dyed to match the bridesmaids' dresses, though it may be a flower that simply complements what the women are wearing and/or their bouquets. The groom wears either a lapel spray to match the bride's bouquet or a traditional boutonniere. The fathers usually have boutonnieres similar to those worn by the groomsmen.

Ceremony Flowers

Flowers are an important part of the ceremony. They accent key points and create atmosphere. If you're getting married in a huge church, you'll need a few large, elaborate arrangements to compete with the surroundings; small displays would simply be swallowed up. Likewise, small accent displays would be a perfect complement to a quaint country church, where large arrangements would over-power the place.

How much of the ceremony site do you want to decorate with flowers? Some brides simply have one large or a few small arrangements placed around the altar. Some also place flowers on the pews, the windows or windowsills, the doors, and anything else that doesn't move.

Christmas and Easter are good times to take note of church flowers. Take a look at how the altar arrangements are presented. Are the flowers on the floor or placed on small tables? Are those tables available to you? If not, can your florist provide something similar? If your church permits you to, take some pictures. This will give you a record of how the church looks when it's all dressed up.

CEREMONY FLOWERS AND DECORATIONS WORKSHEET

Item	Description	Number	Cost
Aisle runner			
Altar flowers			
Garland			
Potted flowers			
Potted plants			
Pews/chair flowers			
Pews/chair bows			
Candelabra			
Candle holders			
Candles			
Unity candle			
Wedding arch			
Columns			
Trellis			
Wreaths for church doors			
Other (list below)			
TOTAL			

Flowers at the Reception

The flowers at the reception are meant to highlight the overall design scheme. Place flowers atop the buffet or wedding cake tables; that will give people something to look at while they think about food. Flowers can also be used to decorate the cake itself.

Depending on the atmosphere of your reception site, hanging plants, small trees, or even topiaries can add a splash of interest to the surroundings. If your budget allows, consider small flower arrangements for the guest tables; they make wonderful centerpieces. Keep in mind that your guests should be able to see one another across the table, so avoid the tall crystal vase with the beautiful flourish of cut flowers and greenery. Keep the arrangements low, especially if your tables are round.

For less formal weddings, small potted plants such as English ivy or philodendrons arranged in decorative baskets make attractive (and affordable!) table decorations. They have the added attraction of being something guests can take home with them and enjoy for years to come.

For a theme wedding (or just for fun), you could add a creative element to your table arrangements. If your theme is "at the beach," place a small arrangement in a wide dish of sand, shells, and colorful sea glass. Fall weddings could be dressed up with bright silk maple leaves, assorted nuts in the shell, Red Delicious apples, and tiny gourds. For a Christmas wedding, arrange flowers in wooden toy sleighs, include gilded or snow-covered pinecones, or perhaps place small, decorated wreaths with candles in the middle of the tables.

Where to Splurge, Where to Save

As you read earlier, flowers are one area of the wedding that can easily break your budget. It's so easy to start saying yes to every arrangement that's offered because they're just so darned pretty.

RECEPTION FLOWERS AND DECORATIONS WORKSHEET

Item	Description	Number	Cost
GUEST TABLES			
Centerpieces			
Garland			
Candles			
HEAD TABLE			
Centerpieces			
Garland			
Candles			
BUFFET TABLE			
Flowers			
Garland			
Decorations			
CAKE TABLE			
Cake top			
Flowers			
Garland			
Decorations			
GUEST BOOK TABLE			
Flowers			
Decorations			
ENVELOPE TABLE			
Flowers			
Decorations			
Candelabra			
Candle holders			
Candles			
Archway			
Columns			
Trellis			
Wreaths			
Garlands			
Potted flowers			
Potted plants			
Hanging plants			
Other *(list below)*			
TOTAL			

Often brides are forced to determine where they want to splurge on flowers and where they wouldn't mind cutting back. Here are some ideas to help you decide:

- **Your bouquet:** splurge. This piece will be a focal point of attention all day long, and it will live on in eternity in your wedding photos.
- **The bridesmaids' flowers:** go halfway. They should complement your bouquet, not compete with it.
- **Groomsmen's boutonnieres:** save. Most men honestly could not care less about the flowers pinned to their lapels. Again, the flowers should complement yours in color, but a carnation will work just as well as an orchid and will be far less expensive.
- **The church flowers:** splurge, especially if you can take those arrangements along to the reception (check with your church; some require that you leave them as a "donation").
- **Flower-girl petals:** these are not inordinately expensive to begin with, but you can make it an even less expensive venture. Craft stores sell packets of artificial flower petals in a variety of colors. Pick up a few to save some cash.

Do It Yourself

You just don't understand all of the fuss surrounding a florist. You can arrange flowers as well as any professional, and you just hate to shell out all that extra money to have someone else complete the task. Oh, and you have lots of time on your hands. Does this sound like you? If you're thinking of tackling your wedding flowers all by yourself, here are some things you should know.

Wholesalers

You'll need to find yourself a good wholesale dealer. What's your best resource? Word of mouth, of course. If you don't know anyone who's ever dealt with a wholesale florist, search online or look in the phone book. Visit wedding fairs, and keep your eyes and ears open. Many wholesalers will even whip up all of your arrangements and deliver the flowers to your church; they just do it for a lower price than the fancy flower shops.

I Want Cheap Flowers . . . Dot-Com

There are also plenty of Internet floral wholesalers that cater to thrifty, crafty brides. In addition to selling flowers at deep discounts, many of these websites also offer instructional videos on how to arrange, tape, and wire your flowers (some also offer chat or e-mail support in case you have a little trouble with your arrangements).

The downside? It's a little risky. The flowers are shipped overnight and are refrigerated so that they arrive fresh on your doorstep, but *what if*. . . ? What if there's a storm, and the plane carrying your flowers is grounded? What if you get the wrong flowers? What if the flowers arrive dead? These are not easy fixes.

The upside to this, of course, is that you can save hundreds of dollars on your wedding flowers, or get more bang for your wedding flower buck. Research the sites carefully; watch the instructional videos to see whether the directions are clear enough for a novice. Take note of whether the site is certified by legitimate wedding associations and/or the Better Business Bureau.

If you decide that this is definitely the way to go, please, please, *please* do a trial run well in advance of the wedding. Order an arrangement. Take note of the arrival time (is it as promised, or several hours late? Promptness is everything in the days leading up to your wedding). Of course, note the condition of the flowers when they arrive, and if you've ordered a DIY piece, then use the

WHOLESALE FLORIST WORKSHEET

Name of wholesaler or website:
....

Contact person:
....

Address:
....

....

Telephone:
....

E-mail:
....

Flowers Ordered	Type	Quantity	Date Ordered	Expected Date of Delivery	Cost

directions to construct it. Using these criteria, you can judge for yourself whether the online vendor is worthy of your wedding dollars.

If you're even a little bit worried about delivery, assembly, or quality, buy your flowers from someone in town instead. It will make your life infinitely less stressful.

The Green Bride

With all of the eco-consciousness going on these days, it's no wonder that some brides are in love with the idea of growing their own wedding flowers. For women who have a green thumb, it's a very admirable as well as cost-saving idea. (For women who can't grow a dandelion, don't even attempt this.) Some tips for creating the self-made bouquet of your dreams:

- Choose flowers you've had luck with in the past. This isn't to say that you can't experiment with something you've never grown as a complementary piece to your bouquet, but you want the healthiest, heartiest blooms anyone has ever seen to be the focal point, and presumably, you know how to grow them.
- Don't skimp on the environment. Get your soil just right for the flowers you're cultivating. Go to your local garden center and have the soil tested; use the fertilizer and other accouterments the experts there recommend. Next year, you can go back to a "good enough" growing foundation; this year it must be perfect.
- Plant more than you need. To be on the safe side, after you figure out which flowers will be used where in your wedding, plant more. There's really no harm in doing so, as you can bet you'll use every bloom that appears.
- Be meticulous with grooming, fertilizing, and watering. Do the research on the flowers you're nurturing, and then follow up with the most exceptional care you can provide.

◆ Clip the day before the wedding, in the morning or in the evening, when the flowers are holding the most water. Make sure
  to use actual flower shears, not your kitchen scissors, which can
  damage the stem before it's actually clipped. Cut at an angle
  and then place in a bucket with flower food. If you're clipping
  several types of flowers, store each in its own bucket.

When you're ready to actually use the flowers, clip them one
more time and then arrange. Flowers going into vases should be
placed into fresh water with floral food.

Alternative Flowers

If you want more flowers than you think you can afford, consider alternative flowers. When done well, silk flower arrangements can be as
beautiful as the real thing—and they even look real. Silk also gives you a
broader choice of colors. While real flowers die quickly, silk flowers can
be kept as decorations or keepsakes long (forever!) after the wedding.

Many brides are using alternative flower options, such as paper
flowers, felt flowers (and other fabrics), and even foraged items.
If you're a crafty DIY bride, you can create unique arrangements
or bouquets in your wedding colors for a signature look on the
big day. If you're not able to create your own flowers, many small
business crafters offer beautiful arrangements that can be tailored
to your individual style—and shipped to your door ahead of time.
Paper flower wholesalers are a great option if you're on a budget.

If you can't bear the thought of not being able to smell the
wedding flowers, but you dig the advantages of alternative options,
compromise. Use live flowers where it's most important, and use
alternative where it doesn't matter. Some brides have two bouquets
made—one real and one alternative. They keep whichever they
prefer and use the other one for the bouquet toss.

CHAPTER 15

Let Them Eat Cake!

THE WEDDING CAKE—it's so pretty, you hate to cut into it and eat it. But alas, your guests will be clamoring for their slices. The wedding cake can be as simple or as ornate as you want it to be. It can be one tier or seven. It can be stacked up on its own layers, or it can incorporate architectural supports. Oh, and your choices of flavors, fillings, and icings are virtually endless.

Types of Cakes

Once upon a time, a wedding cake was white inside and out, but today there are countless options for decoration and consumption. The cake can be garnished with fresh flowers or greenery, and the icing or trimming can be made to match the wedding colors you've selected. The choices for cake flavors, frostings, decorations, and garnishes are plentiful—and tempting. Your cake can be designed any number of ways, including multiple tiers, stacked cakes, multiple sections . . . you could even throw a bridge or a fountain into the mix, too.

Flavors

Bakers have come a long way in a short time. Although many brides choose to have the traditional white or yellow cake, chances are you'll be presented with a long, long list of choices: chocolate, chocolate hazelnut, double chocolate, Italian rum, vanilla, lemon, orange, spice, carrot, cheesecake, citron chiffon, fruitcake, banana, Black Forest, cherry—and the list goes on. You can even choose to have a different flavor for each tier of your cake, just to accommodate the different tastes and needs of your guests.

Fillings

Your baker will probably be able to offer you a wide variety of wedding cake fillings, which may include lemon, custard, raspberry, strawberry, almond crème, chocolate fudge, chocolate mocha, chocolate mousse, pineapple, or cherry nut. And then you may have another opportunity to add a little extra oomph to the cake, with sauces or toppings such as ice cream/sorbet, fresh fruit or fruit sauce, or chocolate.

Cake Toppers

Time was, every wedding cake had a miniature newlywed couple on top of it. It didn't even matter if the couple on top of the cake bore the slightest resemblance to the real-life couple it was representing. It was there to stay. Nowadays, of course, you have other options. You can still go with the bride and groom perched on the top layer of your wedding cake, but it doesn't have to be a perky plastic couple. You can buy a keepsake china or porcelain cake-topper, which will look lovely in your new home after the wedding.

Many brides choose to have fresh (or silk) flowers placed atop their cake, as well as in between tiers. No doubt about it, this is a beautiful alternative to the traditional cake topper. Your baker also can add edible fondant flowers to the cake.

Before You Begin . . .

Reality food shows are all the rage right now, and their amazing confectionary creations are dazzling enough to temporarily blind even the most practical bride. Suddenly, a cake shaped like the Queen Mary, complete with edible lifeboats, or one created in the form of a monster truck with a bride hanging off the back, seem like wildly mainstream choices.

It's fine to have some fun with the theme of your cake; just remember two things:

1. The bakers you see on TV are very stringent in their hiring requirements; that is, their employees are the best-of-the-best and have some very unusual talents. You may not be able to find their counterparts in a small-town setting.
2. Wedding cakes are expensive, period. The more ornate and creative the design, the more you can expect to pay for it.

Meeting the Baker

Depending on where you live, the availability of bakers there, and which season you're planning your wedding for, you may want to contact your baker up to a year in advance, or at least several months before the big day. Bigger, full-service bakeries have more resources available and will be better suited to handle a wedding on short notice. If you want that cute little bakery around the corner to make your wedding cake, talk to them as soon as possible, and be prepared to fork over a big deposit for them to save the date for you. Although this phrase is getting very familiar at this point in your wedding planning, the best way to find a baker is through word of mouth. There's simply no better way of knowing whether a baker can make a delicious and beautiful cake than to talk to someone who has worked with him or her.

The Interview

To get a baker's undivided attention (something you really want and need in order to discuss plans for your wedding cake), make an appointment. You can't pop in during their busiest time and expect that someone will drop everything just to talk business with you. Also, by calling ahead, you're giving the bakery time to prepare batters and icings for your approval.

If you want your cake to include your wedding colors, bring a swatch of fabric with you. If there's a definite style of cake that you're after, bring a picture or sketch. You'll also need to bring along the names and numbers of your florist and photographer, as well as all the relevant information regarding your reception site (location, contact name and number, and directions). Here are some issues to address with the baker:

1. **Size.** You'll have to know how many guests you're inviting in order to nail down what size cake you'll need.

2. **Flavor, filling, icing.** You'll be given a list to choose from. If you want different flavors on different tiers, ask your baker if he can do this for you.
3. **Specialty.** Does this baker have a specialty cake? Can you taste it?
4. **Backup plans.** If your cake should suffer an unforeseen tragedy on the morning of your wedding, will this bakery have another cake ready for you?

Cake Costs

Of course, the other big issue you'll want to discuss is price. Most bakeries will base their prices on a plain cake with buttercream frosting—*each slice* will cost you X dollars. (For example, if you're having 200 guests and the cake is $3 a slice, you're looking at a $600 cake.) From there, you'll add to the price of each slice with each upgrade. Fillings will cost you so much per slice, while rolled fondant frosting will cost you so much more per slice. And if you want any fancy design work on your cake, you're looking at paying even *more*. (And you always wondered how the cost of wedding cakes can spiral completely out of control?) If you decide to incorporate pillars, bridges, or fountains, you'll probably be charged a rental fee for these supports.

Delivery is usually included in the price of the cake. However, each bakery has its own specific delivery limitations (a radius of thirty miles from the bakery, for example). If your reception falls outside that area, an extra charge may be added. Sometimes, if the design is delicate, the cake will have to be transported in pieces and assembled on-site—this may incur another charge for labor. Also, some bakeries have minimum order amounts.

You Take the Cake!

Make sure the baker arrives at the reception in time to set up the cake before the guests arrive. As we just discussed, multi-tiered cakes may need to be transported in sections and assembled at the reception site. Unless you want this phenomenon to be part of the reception entertainment, make arrangements with the site coordinator to allow the baker plenty of time to get in early and do his thing. And remember to touch base with the coordinator about where the cake will be placed. Though traffic patterns and simple space restrictions may dictate where the cake goes, if the background will be unsightly for your pictures, your photographer may be able to bring a backdrop of his own.

Saving Cake

You may want to preserve the top layer of your cake for tradition's sake. There is a tradition of freezing the summit of your wedding cake so that you and your husband can thaw it out and enjoy it on your first anniversary. Your baker will probably address this issue with you. If he doesn't, and you're interested in saving the cake, make sure you bring it up. The smallest (top) layer is generally made of a special, freezer-friendly type of cake (regular wedding cake only lasts three months or so in a freezer); hence, your baker needs to know that you want the cake to make it a full year.

Cut It Down

Rest assured, there *are* ways to cut costs. Your decorated cake does not have to serve all of the guests. Save money by ordering a smaller decorated cake, along with a supplemental sheet cake (which is kept in the kitchen, not on display) to feed your guests. On the other hand, if dessert is already included on your wedding menu, there's really no need for a wedding cake except for the traditional cake-cutting ceremony. If that's the case, you can cut costs by making it as small and simple as possible.

The Groom's Cake

In the very old days, the groom's cake was a dark fruitcake—a symbol of the sweet life that lay ahead for the newlyweds. The slices were packaged in monogrammed boxes as a wedding favor for each guest. According to the superstition, if a single woman slept with the cake box under her pillow that night, she'd dream of the man she was to marry. Of course, as with all wedding traditions, this one has evolved with time.

The groom's cake is supposed to give the groom *his* moment in the spotlight, so it should reflect his interests. If he's a hockey player, order a cake in the shape of a hockey stick or a puck; if he's an outdoorsy type, the cake can depict him hiking or fishing. The groom's cake is supposed to be a little more fun than the wedding cake, so nothing is off-limits.

The groom's cake can be served at the reception, but you may want to serve it at the rehearsal. You can order a groom's cake from the same baker who is doing your wedding cake—and if you want to keep it a secret from the groom, that's all right, too.

Let Them Eat Pastries!

There are alternatives to the traditional wedding cake. Here are a few ideas:

- **Individually decorated cakes.** Each guest gets his or her own mini wedding cake.
- **Decorated cupcakes.** These can be served individually, or stacked to resemble one big cake.
- **Bride and groom cookies.** Your hair color and dress style can be copied onto a cookie!

BAKER WORKSHEET

Name of bakery:
....
Address:
....
Website:
....
Telephone:
....
Contact:
....
Hours:
....
Directions:
....

....

APPOINTMENTS

Date: Time:
....
Date: Time:
....
Date: Time:
....
Order date:
....
Delivery/Pick-up date: Time:
....
Delivery/Pick-up instructions:
....

COST

Total amount due:
....
Amount of deposit: Date:
....
Balance due: Date:
....
Sales tax included?   ◯ Yes   ◯ No
....
Terms of cancellation:
....

....
Notes:
....

And something that has always been part and parcel of the big Italian wedding for many years, the pastry table, is becoming a staple at other weddings these days. You may decide to offer your guests a variety of desserts immediately following dinner, or you may simply choose to set up a pastry table later in the evening, for your guests who have worn themselves out boogying on the dance floor.

The Baker in the Bridal Dress

Some brides are confectionary experts, and they just cannot fathom shelling out hundreds or thousands of dollars for a dessert they could create themselves. And if you are truly a baking bandit, you're right—you can save a boatload of money by creating your own wedding cake.

First and foremost, making your own cake means you are without the benefit of a bakery storing and delivering it for you. You'll need to find someone willing to transport the cake to the venue for you, so think of some people you know with large trucks or vans. Contact local bakeries and inquire if they would be willing to work out a deal to transport your cake in their vehicles—it's worth a shot!

Presumably, any bride who would consider baking her own cake knows that it will be a time commitment. You can store many cake layers for up to two weeks in the freezer; fillings and frostings can generally be refrigerated for up to one week. But there will be trial runs, not just of the cake/filling/frosting themselves but also of the decorations. Will you be working with fondant? Fresh flowers? Beads, pearls, crystals? Start your sketches and practice runs at least two months before the wedding. You want that cake to steal the show, not detract from your lovely day. You can find countless recipes for wedding cakes online; simply search for the flavors/shapes you're looking for. And be sure to check out www .cakewrecks.com for a good laugh.

WEDDING CAKE WORKSHEET

Item	Description	Cost
WEDDING CAKE		
Size		
Shape		
Number of tiers		
Number cake will serve		
Flavor of cake		
Flavor of filling		
Flavor of icing		
Icing decorations		
Cake top		
Cake decorations		
Other		
GROOM'S CAKE		
Size		
Shape		
Number cake will serve		
Flavor		
Icing		
Cake top		
Cake decorations		
Other		
OTHER		
Cake serving set		
Cake boxes		
Delivery charge		
Other *(list below)*		
TOTAL		

CHAPTER 16

Getting There

MOST BRIDES PICTURE THEMSELVES arriving in style at the door of the wedding site. If you're going to need a ride to the ceremony, you'll need to start looking as soon as possible. And if you're thinking about ditching the limo in favor of a plane ride to a destination wedding, you might be in a quandary as to how you're going to get your dress there on time (not to mention your guests).

Limousine Luxury

Limousines are the most common mode of wedding transportation. Though it may not be as original or exciting as arriving in, say, a fighter plane, showing up in a well-kept limousine has its perks. You can seat ten (or more) people comfortably, serve yourself from the bar, and have a chauffeur at your beck and call. A big shiny limousine is also impressive enough to instill awe in the occupants of those boring regular cars who are sitting next to you in traffic.

Must You Hire a Fleet?

If your transportation budget is on the smallish side, you might have to make some compromises. Some couples hire just one limousine. Usually this necessitates an intricate series of passenger exchanges on the wedding day. Here's how it works: The bride gets the first ride in the limo, which transports her and her parents to the ceremony site. It could then pick up the groom and deliver him to the site. After the ceremony, the bride returns to the limousine with her groom, and the two of them ride to the reception. (Alternate scenario: if the ceremony site is close enough to where the bride and bridesmaids are getting ready, the limousine can make its first trip to the ceremony site with the bridesmaids, then come back for the bride.) Depending on how long you have rented the limousine for, the newlyweds might also be driven in style to their hotel after the reception—or perhaps to the airport to begin their honeymoon.

More Cars

If your budget is stretchable, you might want to rent one or two additional limousines to transport attendants and possibly your parents. This not only saves you the hassle of coordinating other transportation for them but also leaves them thinking you're really swell.

Your attendants will pile into waiting limos after the ceremony. Taking pictures will go more smoothly if everyone arrives at the site together, and you won't have to worry about any attendants getting lost on the way to the reception. Just make sure that no one gets left behind at the site where you've taken your photos. To avoid this possibility, it might be a good idea to assign attendants to limos by pairs (each bridesmaid and her groomsman)—particularly if one of your friends is prone to a mishap like this.

Logistics

If you're hiring only one car to take you to the church and the reception, how are you going to get to the hotel afterward? And how are your bridesmaids going to get home if they weren't accompanied to the wedding?

Your bridesmaids are technically on their own after the reception is over. However, you can always ask a friend or relative if she would be willing to chauffeur any attendants who are stuck for a ride home after the limo leaves at the end of the evening.

You and your groom will have to make sure that either someone will drive you to your final destination for the evening or one of you has made arrangements to leave your own car in the parking lot at the reception. Oh, and make sure you don't lose track of the keys. It would be a real bummer to be stuck in the parking lot after everyone else has left and the reception hall has locked its doors for the evening!

Advance Reservations

Generally speaking, it's never too early to look into your transportation options. If you're getting married during the peak season (April through October), get on the ball right away. It's not uncommon for limos to be booked a year in advance; many companies will even take reservations up to a year and a half before an event. If you're unsure about your area (for example, if limos don't seem to be very popular, or there just aren't a lot of weddings), call some companies and ask for their recommendations.

Keep in mind that May and June are also big prom and graduation months, so limos will be in high demand for these events. As soon as you start *thinking* about your wedding-day transportation, get moving on booking your vehicles.

Finding the Right Limo

Picture this. It's your wedding day. You're all dressed and ready to go, and all you need now is the limousine to roll up and get you to the church on time. But it doesn't. Or it does come, but it's covered by a dusty haze and has mud caked on its three remaining hubcaps. Or it looks snazzy enough on the outside, but inside, the television and bar you requested are nowhere to be found. You wouldn't mind any of that, would you?

Clearly, you'll want to do everything you can to prevent problems like these ahead of time. A recently married friend or relative may be able to recommend a reliable limousine service with good cars and thereby save you a lot of legwork. But if you're not that lucky, get yourself out there, look at the cars, and ask some questions.

Deal with the Owner

Try to find a company that owns its limousines. Owners are more likely to keep track of a car's maintenance and whereabouts. (You do not want to ride in a limo that has seen its share of unauthorized excursions.)

Make sure you verify a service's license and insurance coverage. Get references. Verify that its chauffeurs show up on time, are courteous, and don't have bad habits like driving into trees.

Inspect all the cars. Does the fleet look modern and up-to-date, or are the cars looking like they might be on their last legs? Are there obvious scratches or dents on the cars? (There shouldn't be.) When you get in to inspect the vehicles, are the interior surfaces spotless? (They should be.) Are the windows clean? Do the cars smell like smoke? Is there enough room for your groom and his linebacker buddies to spread out without crushing any crinolines? Is there enough headroom for the gigantic hairdos your bridesmaids will be sporting?

Most importantly, does this company have the kind of limo you want? If you're looking at a pink limo and you don't want anything but a black one, are there other cars available? Don't take a company's word that it can get you a black stretch limo with black leather interior. You need to see it with your own eyes—and don't sign anything until you have.

How Much?

Most limousine services charge by the hour. Unfortunately for you, the clock starts the second the driver leaves the base, not the moment he or she begins driving you around. (If you can find a service that's based near your home and the festivities, you'll save yourself some money.) Most companies have package deals with a specific number of hours included in the price—but you need to understand what's included. A three-hour package might sound like more than enough time, because you know you're not going to be sitting in that limo for three hours. But if there's a delay between the ceremony and the reception (if you're getting married at one o'clock and your reception is at five, for example) you're going to need at least five hours to be on the safe side.

Find out the exact costs and exactly what you'll be getting for your money. Does the limo company provide champagne? Ice? Glasses? A red carpet? Some limo companies can add extras like balloons or flowers. Some also offer a "runner" service, which means that you can keep the driver "on call" to run home any guests who have had too much to drink at the reception.

Sign Here

Once you decide on a limousine service, get all the details finalized in a written contract. It should specify the type of car, additional options and services you will need, the expected length of service, the date, and the time. If there's a specific limo you just have to have (it's the only one with two sunroofs, or it's the only one with satellite radio), ask the owner to specify it on the contract. Some limo companies have vanity plates on their cars for this very purpose.

Ask about contingencies. If you're choosing the company's top-of-the-line car and something happens to it, what then? Get this in writing, also.

Don't Drive Your Driver Crazy

A strange thing sometimes happens to brides, grooms, and their attendants. They sometimes feel as though they are the stars of some strange nighttime soap opera, one where the women are wearing bridesmaid dresses—or they're suddenly transported back to their prom night. Either way, they feel they are entitled to heap abuse upon the chauffeur.

Be kind to your driver. He isn't being paid to be treated like a servant. He's just there to provide a service for you—namely, driving the car. If your attendants are giving the guy a hard time, step in. You never know when a chauffeur might snap and leave you stranded in the middle of nowhere while your reception goes on without you.

The chauffeur's tip, usually 10 to 20 percent of the bill, is sometimes included in the fee, but read the fine print of your contract to find out for sure. You don't want to stiff someone who has provided you with a good service and who has helped make

DRIVER'S CHECKLIST WORKSHEET

Give a copy of this to each driver.

Vehicle:
....

Driver:
....

Date:
....

Name of bride and groom:
....

1. Place of pick-up: Arrival time:
....

Names of passenger(s):
....

Address:
....

....

Telephone:
....

Directions:
....

....

Special instructions:
....

....

2. Place of pick-up: Arrival time:
....

Names of passenger(s):
....

Address:
....

....

Telephone:
....

Directions:
....

....

Special instructions:
....

....

....

....

3. Place of pick-up: Arrival time:
....
Names of passenger(s):
....
Address:
....

....
Telephone:
....
Directions:
....

....
Special instructions:
....

....
4. Ceremony location: Arrival time:
....
Names of passenger(s):
....
Address:
....

....
Telephone:
....
Directions:
....

....
Special instructions:
....

....
5. Reception location: Arrival time:
....
Names of passenger(s):
....
Address:
....

....
Telephone:
....
Directions:
....

....
Special instructions:
....

your day run (or ride) smoothly. By the same token, if you are dissatisfied with the service your chauffeur provides, speak up!

Other Vehicles

Limos aren't your thing, you say? Sure, they're fine for other brides, but you're looking for a something different—but not crazy-different? Fortunately for you, there are many other options. Some of the most popular, and easy to find, alternatives are included in this section.

Horse and Carriage

This is romance on wheels. No matter what the season, there's no sight more beautiful or that conjures up a more royal image, than a bride riding to the church in a horse-drawn carriage. If you're planning a winter wedding, obviously you will, at the very least, have to invest in a warm wrap. In areas that are hit hard by winter storms, you may want to leave the carriage out of your planning altogether. Better to play it safe during this particular season and hire something with a motor, snow tires—and a heater.

Shuttles and Trolleys

If you're not concerned with the aesthetics of your ride, an option that's gaining popularity is renting a shuttle bus for your wedding party. There are plenty of seats for everyone, plenty of room for purses and coats. This option encourages a fun, casual atmosphere onboard.

To be fair, you can't expect this vehicle to be spit-shined, nor should you expect to feel as though you've stepped into anything resembling a limo. This is definitely a functional vehicle. Your entire wedding party fits inside and can move about the cabin at will, and that spells good times for you. Period.

Trolleys offer the same kind of space as a shuttle bus, but in a classier package. Many trolley rides are open-air affairs, but in colder climates, most offer some kind of protection from the winter elements.

Sleek Rides

Are you the white Rolls-Royce type? Perhaps a silver Bentley would suit you best. If you've got some extra cash on hand, go all out: Snag an Excalibur. It will make for a truly unforgettable shot in your wedding video. Many limousine companies also have a few classic cars on their lots. You can look in your phone or online directory under "livery." You don't have to squeeze your attendants into this car with you—you can hire a limo or SUV just for them.

Free Ride

If for some reason you are unable to rent wedding transportation, look around for family members or friends who have nice big cars they'd be willing to lend you. Some car buffs are likely to be horrified at the idea of someone else behind the wheel of their baby. If that's the case, you can always ask them to play the part of chauffeur for the day.

The only requirement here is that the cars have to be clean. You should pay for the prewedding car wash and detailing. And be sure to remember your generous friends with a little gift and a full tank of gas.

Transporting the Entire Wedding

If you're planning a wedding on a Caribbean island or somewhere overseas, you're going to be faced with much larger transportation issues. Getting yourself there is the easy part—but what about your dress?! If you're inviting guests, are you expected to pay for their transportation, too?

Destination Weddings Know-How

A wedding on a small island, or at a mountain resort, or on the shores of the Mediterranean might be what you're after. The guest list for a destination wedding tends to be small, including only the people you're closest to. The ceremony is the focus of the trip. When all's said and done, you don't need to hop a flight to start your honeymoon.

Obviously, a lot of planning has to go into a wedding that you're taking on the road. Find yourself a good travel agent. She will know the ins and outs of all-inclusive resorts, and will also know the requirements of any foreign country where you're thinking of saying your vows.

Of course, the Internet is also a great tool for researching your destination, but it should be used in conjunction with a travel agent. As good as the Internet is, you want to talk to someone who either has been to this place him- or herself or knows someone else who has. *Word of mouth*—you can't escape it.

Pack Your Wedding Bags!

Beautiful, expensive dresses don't like to be smushed into suitcases. They aren't really designed for the same kind of abuse that your weekend clothing or even your travel-friendly business suits can take. When transporting your wedding dress, you can't be careful enough. If you can arrange to have the dress packed and shipped, do it. Courier companies are much better equipped than your average airline to handle fragile items and to deliver them in one piece, in a timely manner. If you're planning a wedding at a resort that specializes in destination weddings, there will probably be an on-site coordinator you will be able to work with who will know exactly how to steam those inevitable wrinkles out of the dress on your wedding day.

TRANSPORTATION WORKSHEET

Name of company:
....

Address:
....

Website:
....

Telephone:
....

Contact: Hours:
....

Directions:
....

....

Services provided:
....

....

Number of vehicles rented:
....

Description:
....

....

Cost per hour:
....

Minimum number of hours:
....

Overtime cost:
....

Hours of rental:
....

Name of driver(s):

COST

Total amount due:
....

Amount of deposit: Date:
....

Balance due: Date:
....

Sales tax included?   ◯ Yes   ◯ No
....

Terms of cancellation:
....

....

Notes:
....

....

Of course, you may start to see the logic in forgoing a big, frilly dress when you're confronted with the reality of transporting it. For a beach wedding, you can absolutely go the less formal route and choose a gauze or cotton dress or sarong. (These fabrics make more fashion sense in a tropical climate than do satin or brocade, anyway.)

The Guests

Let's say that you and your groom chose a destination wedding because you've always dreamed of standing on the beach while saying "I do," but you also want your family and friends to come along. Are you expected to pay for *their* transportation or lodging? If you're including attendants in the ceremony, their hotel bill is your responsibility, according to traditional wedding etiquette. If you can afford their airfare, that's a nice touch. Everyone else is on their own, though that's not to say that you can't take everyone out for an island barbecue one evening.

To be fair, you can't expect that everyone you invite will be able to make it to a destination event. It is a costly proposition, and the folks on your guest list might have other things that they'd like (or have) to do with their cash and their vacation days.

DESTINATION WEDDING: TRAVEL INFO WORKSHEET

GUESTS

....

....

....

....

....

....

....

....

....

....

....

....

....

DATES OF TRAVEL

Arriving at destination:
....

Departing from destination:

FLIGHT INFORMATION

Airline:
....

Phone:
....

Website:
....

Date and time of reservations:
....

Seat numbers:
....

Confirmation number:
....

CAR RENTAL INFORMATION

Phone:
....

Website:
....

Date and time of reservations:
....

Make and model:
....

Confirmation number:

RESORT/CRUISE LINE CONTACT INFORMATION

Phone:
....

Website:
....

E-mail:
....

Date and time of reservations:
....

Number of rooms reserved:
....

Confirmation number:

CEREMONY SITE INFORMATION

Site name:
....

Website:
....

Date and time of reservations:
....

Officiant:
....

Officiant's phone:
....

Officiant's e-mail:

RECEPTION SITE INFORMATION

Site name:
....

Website:
....

Date and time of reservations:
....

Contact person:
....

Contact person's phone:
....

Contact person's e-mail:
....

FLOWERS/DECORATIONS

Type of flowers:
....

Cost:
....

Date and time of reservations:
....

Florist's phone:
....

Florist's e-mail:

MUSIC

Musicians/DJ:
....

Cost:
....

Musicians/DJ's e-mail:
....

Musicians/DJ's phone:
....

Date and time of reservations:

ADDITIONAL INFORMATION

....

....

....

....

....

....

....

....

....

....

....

....

....

CHAPTER 17

Little Legalities

LEGAL DETAILS MAY NOT SOUND EXCITING, but certain minor details, such as deciding on your married name and procuring the marriage license, need to be addressed. There's also a bigger issue that may warrant some attention in your relationship: the prenuptial agreement. These aren't necessarily fun tasks, but taking care of them gets you one step closer to the altar.

Choosing Your Name

Have you ever really stopped to think about how much you like (or dislike) your own name? Maybe since you've accepted your fiancé's proposal, you've started thinking about how much you really love (love!) your name. This is the name you went through school with, the name you built your career with, and the name everyone knows you by. How can you kiss it off? On the other hand, maybe your last name is ten syllables long, or no one ever pronounces or spells it right, and you can't wait to change it. Easy decision.

If you're in a tizzy over what your married name should be, remember that these days it isn't a societal issue when a women goes against the long-standing tradition of changing her name to her husband's.

The Name Remains the Same

If you decide to keep your name, you've made life easy for yourself in many regards. At the same time, there *are* a few situations that will inevitably pop up, and you'll want to be prepared for them.

His Family

If you decide to keep your maiden name, you should be sensitive to how your in-laws might react. Explain the reason for your decision (for example, that you've already established a career identity with your maiden name) and emphasize that your decision in no way reflects a lack of respect for their family. Ask your spouse to voice his support of your decision.

The World

Until people are aware of your decision to keep your maiden name, you may find yourself in situations in which you are incorrectly addressed by your husband's surname. You may well be dealing with correcting people for the rest of your life.

If someone should call you by your husband's surname, don't make him or her feel like a terrible person. It's a common assumption (yes, even in the twenty-first century). You can either let it pass or politely correct the person, depending on how important the issue is to you. As a way to avoid awkwardness, take the initiative and introduce yourself: "Hi, I'm Jennifer Andrews, Richard Miller's wife." (Or "I'm Jennifer Andrews; Richard Miller is my husband.")

Kids

Some women who keep their maiden name will still choose to use their husband's surname for their children. It's not an uncommon occurrence these days for kids to have different surnames than their parents, for a variety of reasons. Chances are, whatever decision you make about your surname and your kids' surname won't seem all that unusual when they enter school.

Little Changes

For many brides, the issue of the name change (or no change) is a game of eeny-meeny-miny-mo. They like their own name, but they also really want to take their husband's name, as a show of solidarity or because they simply want to. Fortunately, there are multiple options to accommodate just about any name combination or situation.

If you'd kind of like to take your husband's name, but you don't want to completely abandon your own, consider these options:

◆ **Use your maiden name as your middle name, and your husband's surname as your surname.** (In this case, Jennifer

Andrews marrying Richard Miller becomes Jennifer Andrews Miller.)

- **Hyphenate the two last names.** Jennifer Andrews-Miller. That little dash means that the two separate last names are now joined to make one (like a marriage). Your husband can use this name, too.
- **Take your two last names and create an entirely new surname for both of you to use.** Andrews and Miller could be combined into Andler or Milland, for example.

Some women choose to take their husband's name legally and socially but continue to use their maiden name for business.

If you've decided to take on a new name, you'll have some paperwork to deal with. It's not quite as easy as it should be, but not quite the daunting task it sounds like it might be, either. Signing your name on the marriage license is proof of your new name. Now you just have to inform the appropriate people. Wait until you've received a copy of your marriage license before you attempt to change your name on accounts or documents. In many instances (when changing your name on bank accounts, for example), you'll need proof that you are who you say you are, and your marriage license is confirmation of your new title.

Now you've got to inform relevant organizations that you no longer are who you used to be. Your first concerns should be these:

- Driver's license
- Social Security card
- Credit cards
- Bank accounts, loans, and so on
- Car registration
- Passport
- Insurance

BRIDE'S NAME AND ADDRESS CHANGE WORKSHEET

Information to Be Changed	Name of Institution	Notified of Name Change?	Notified of Change of Address?	Notified of Change in Marital Status?
401k accounts				
Automotive insurance				
Bank accounts				
Billing accounts				
Car registration				
Club memberships				
Credit cards				
Dentist				
Doctors				
Driver's license				
Employment records				
Homeowner's/ Renter's insurance				
IRA accounts				
Leases				
Life insurance				
Loans				
Medical insurance				
Other insurance accounts				
Passport				
Pension plan records				
Post office				
Property titles				
Safety deposit box				
School records				
Social Security				
Stocks and bonds				
Subscriptions				
Telephone listing				
Voter registration records				
Wills/trusts				
Other				

GROOM'S NAME AND ADDRESS CHANGE WORKSHEET

Information to Be Changed	Name of Institution	Notified of Name Change?	Notified of Change of Address?	Notified of Change in Marital Status?
401k accounts				
Automotive insurance				
Bank accounts				
Billing accounts				
Car registration				
Club memberships				
Credit cards				
Dentist				
Doctors				
Driver's license				
Employment records				
Homeowner's/ Renter's insurance				
IRA accounts				
Leases				
Life insurance				
Loans				
Medical insurance				
Other insurance accounts				
Passport				
Pension plan records				
Post office				
Property titles				
Safety deposit box				
School records				
Social Security				
Stocks and bonds				
Subscriptions				
Telephone listing				
Voter registration records				
Wills/trusts				
Other				

NEWSPAPER WEDDING ANNOUNCEMENT WORKSHEET

To appear in _____ newspaper on _____ *(date)*.

Name(s) of sender: _____

Address: _____

_____

Contact person: _____

Phone number: _____ E-mail: _____

_____ and _____

(bride's first, middle, and maiden names)   *(groom's first, middle, and last names)*

were married at _____ in _____ .

(name of church or synagogue)   *(town)*

The bride, _____ ,

(optional: name change information, for example, "will continue to use her surname")

is the daughter of Mr. and Mrs. _____ of _____ .

(bride's parents' names)   *(their city, if out of town)*

She graduated from _____ and is a/an _____

(optional: name of college or university)   *(job title)*

at _____ . The bridegroom, son of Mr. and Mrs. _____

(name of employer)   *(groom's parents' names)*

of _____ , graduated from _____ and

(their city, if out of town)   *(optional: name of college or university)*

is a/an _____ at _____ . The couple will live in

(job title)   *(name of employer)*

_____ after a trip to _____ .

(city or town)   *(honeymoon location)*

Marriage License Requirements

The criteria for obtaining a marriage license vary not only from state to state but often from county to county within a single state. Before you head off to get your marriage license, find out how long the license will be valid. There's no rule of thumb here. In some regions, the license is valid for several weeks, while in others it never expires.

General Concerns

Regardless of where you get married, you should be aware of some guidelines for the marriage license. Every state addresses the following issues:

- **Paperwork.** You'll need some sort of valid identification (birth certificate, driver's license, proof of age, proof of citizenship). You must provide proof of divorce or annulment in the case of a second marriage.
- **Fee.** Every state charges a fee, and thankfully, most are not outrageous. Be aware that many states will accept only cash as payment.
- **Minimum age.** If you're fourteen and looking to get married in most states, you're out of luck, unless your parents agree to it. In most areas, you need to be at least eighteen.
- **Waiting period.** Again, this varies by state. Some states require a waiting period of several days between obtaining the license and saying "I do." In other areas, you can get the license and get married on the same day.

Your best bet is to make a call to your county clerk's office. There's a lot of information on the Internet, but not all of it is up-to-date. In this case it's best to talk to a human who has the most up-to-date information on the matter.

License Limitations

Having a marriage license doesn't mean you are legally married. It means you have the state's permission to get married. To be valid and binding, the license has to be signed by a religious or civil official, so once you have the license in your possession, don't lose it.

When the ceremony rolls around, you'll give the license to your officiant. The officiant simply signs the license after the completion of the ceremony and sends it back to the proper state office. *Now* you're married. (Yay!)

The Lowdown on Prenuptial Agreements

The issue of prenuptial agreements is a hot-button topic among brides. Some feel that prenups are the most unromantic and depressing things ever. Other brides feel that prenups are worth the time and effort needed to ensure smooth sailing into the future. If you don't even want to acknowledge the existence of these contracts, then go ahead and skip this section. If, on the other hand, you're even a little interested in this sort of thing, your information is here.

What Are They For?

Prenups aren't just for people with lots of money. They're also used to protect assets such as family businesses from being attacked by lawyers if there is marital discord down the road. A common reason for having a prenuptial agreement is to protect the interests of children from a previous marriage. Many parents want to make sure that their children's inheritance is never an issue in the event of divorce or death.

An interesting fact: the law in most states dictates that prenuptial agreements have to be fair to both parties. Take a wife who is supporting her husband while he goes to medical school, for example. The husband can't say that in the event of a divorce, he keeps every penny of his earnings, because the wife contributed to his success. The wife might request a prenup to protect her future interests should the marriage dissolve.

What's Addressed?

Prenups basically cover the assets, debts, and incomes of each spouse. They might also address any inheritances that either spouse receives during the marriage (who gets to spend it?), tax issues (will you file joint returns, or separate ones?), living arrangements, and children from a previous marriage (it's common for the kids—rather than the second or third husband or wife—to be named as benefactors of a will).

A prenup should include the following elements:

- Full, written disclosure of the assets and liabilities of each party
- Reasonable terms
- Adequate time for the parties to review the terms with their own lawyers

MARRIAGE LICENSE CHECKLIST WORKSHEET

To file for a marriage license, you will need one or more of the following. (Check your state and county guidelines for the specific requirements in your area.)

Valid Identification

❍ Driver's license

❍ Birth certificate

❍ Military ID card

❍ Social Security card

❍ Passport

❍ Other: _____

❍ Proof of divorce or annulment *(if applicable)*

❍ Application fee: $ _____

Filed for marriage license on:

....

(date)

....

(date)

Location where marriage license is stored for safekeeping:

....

....

....

....

....

....

PRENUPTIAL AGREEMENT CHECKLIST WORKSHEET

Name of law firm/attorneys:
....

Address:
....

Telephone:
....

E-mail:
....

Meetings:
....

Date: .... Time: ....

Date: .... Time: ....

Bride's assets   **Bride's liabilities**

....

....

....

....

Groom's assets   **Groom's liabilities**

....

....

....

....

SPECIFIC ISSUES TO BE ADDRESSED IN AGREEMENT

Bride's concerns:
....

....

....

Groom's concerns:
....

....

....

CHAPTER 18

The Rehearsal

IF YOU'RE EXPECTING your wedding rehearsal to go something like the final dress rehearsal for a Broadway play, it probably won't. You'll probably have the jitters that echo an opening-night panic attack, but your rehearsal will be much less dramatic and nerve-wracking than you might think. The rehearsal is mainly a chance for the officiant to meet your wedding party and to acquaint everyone with the basics of the ceremony. And yes, it's very exciting.

Who Should Be There?

Who (besides you and your groom) should attend the rehearsal? That one's easy: the officiant, every member of the wedding party, the father of the bride (to practice his suave look as he makes his way down the aisle, of course), Scripture readers and candle lighters, and any children taking part in the ceremony should all be included. Basically, you should invite anyone who is involved as more than just a guest. You want to make sure everyone knows what happens when, and who's doing what where.

You can invite the florist to discuss final issues of flower placement. You might also want to arrange for featured soloists or musicians to attend the rehearsal. Your readers should check with the officiant to make sure the version of Scripture they've been practicing in front of the mirror at home is in fact the one being used in the ceremony. (Sometimes the wording differs from Bible to Bible, depending on the version. The officiant will know for sure which version will be used in the ceremony.)

Remember, this is your chance to iron out last-minute details and resolve remaining questions. Though even this may not be enough to truly calm your nerves, try to get everything straight at the rehearsal. Make sure that everything is ready and that all of the participants know what's expected of them.

The Final Run-Through

The rehearsal is usually held a night or two before the wedding at the ceremony site. If that time is inconvenient for any of your key players, reschedule it for another time, preferably during the week before the wedding. (If it's held too far in advance of the wedding, people may forget what they've rehearsed.) Some brides are requesting—and being given—rehearsal dates several nights before the wedding, for the logical reason that on the eve of the wedding itself, the bride and groom are often on edge and/or incredibly busy.

After a brief overview of what's included in the ceremony, the officiant will talk everyone through a quick practice run, starting with the processional, which is at the very beginning of the ceremony, when the first bridesmaid takes her first step down that long aisle.

The Processional

Part of the reason that you have the rehearsal is to determine what's allowed in the processional in your particular church. Some churches encourage the bridesmaids and groomsmen to traipse down the aisle together. Other churches prefer to have the bridesmaids walk alone and have the groomsmen stand at the altar with the groom. Still others do a sort of hybrid of the two. The bridesmaids start out by themselves, and the groomsmen meet them halfway and escort them to the front of the church. Your officiant or the site coordinator will instruct your attendants on which is their preferred method.

Which bridesmaid leads the pack? It's up to you. Either pick names from a hat, or start sorting by height. For large weddings with many bridesmaids, you can send them to the altar in pairs. The honor attendant (the maid or matron of honor) is the last maid to walk down the aisle, followed by the ringbearer and flower girl.

After the flower girl has left her station at the back of the church, it's your turn, on the arm of the person who is giving you away (or by yourself, if you choose, or escorted by both parents), followed by pages (if you have them), who carry the bride's train.

Jewish Orthodox, Conservative, and Reform processions vary according to the families' preferences, devoutness, and local custom. A traditional religious Jewish processional may begin with the rabbi and cantor, with the cantor on the rabbi's right, followed by the groomsmen walking one by one, and then the best man. The groom then walks between his mother, on his right, and his father, on his left. The bridesmaids then walk one by one, followed by the maid of honor, the page, and the flower girl. The bride is the last to enter, with her mother on her right and her father on her left.

Giving the Bride Away

Traditionally, the father of the bride gives the bride away. But sometimes death, divorce, or other issues change people's circumstances. When faced with the loss of a father, many unmarried women wonder who will give them away at their wedding.

If your father has passed away, do whatever feels most comfortable to you. If your mother has remarried and you are close to your stepfather, he may be a good choice. Otherwise, a brother, a grandfather, a special uncle, or a close family friend can do the honor. Some brides walk down the aisle with their mothers or even with the groom. Others choose to walk without an escort. Keep in mind that whomever you choose will sit in the front pew with your mother during the ceremony (unless you choose your groom, of course).

If your parents are divorced and both parents are remarried, your decision will depend on your preference and family situation. To avoid risking civil war, take care to somehow include both men in the proceedings. If you've remained close to your father, you may prefer that he fulfill his traditional role, while your stepfather does a reading. Or perhaps you'll ask them both to escort you down the aisle. Often in Jewish ceremonies both parents, even when divorced, walk the bride down the aisle.

Many second-time brides walk down the aisle with their grooms, or with one of their children. However, it's also appropriate for the bride's father to escort her again, or for her to walk alone.

You may decide to do away with this tradition altogether. If so, there are options that you should discuss with your officiant. Instead of asking, "Who gives this woman . . . ?" he or she may ask, "Who blesses this union?" Your father may respond, "Her mother and I do," and take his seat next to your mother. It is also entirely appropriate for both parents to respond, "We do." In this case, your mother should also stand up when the officiant presents the question.

Again, a brother, uncle, grandfather, or close friend can stand in if you do not have a positive relationship with your father. In this case, the person who walked you down the aisle can give you away, or if you are uncomfortable with the idea of being "given away," the officiant can ask the entire congregation, "Who supports this couple?" To which the group can respond, "We do."

The Ceremony

You'll have a quick run-through of the ceremony, which probably will not include the music but probably will include your readers and gift presenters (if any) practicing their parts. You want everyone to know where the heck they're going, after all.

Quick means quick. Your readers may not even present the readings during the rehearsal, and the gift presenters will obviously not be presenting any bread and wine. You and your groom will stand in your places as your officiant goes over the nuptials with you. He will remind you of the appropriate responses to the questions, and if you're going to be reciting your own vows, your officiant will let you know when you'll be expected to speak.

Your officiant may seem nitpicky in saying that you should be facing the groom more, or that you should enunciate, but he has performed countless ceremonies and knows the drill. He also knows the quirks of the acoustics of the place—and whether the people in the third row will have a hard time hearing the vows. *You*, on the other hand, are a novice at this. Heed the advice you're given.

In addition, your honor attendants will be instructed as to their special duties during the ceremony. For instance, your maid of honor will need to take your flowers at a certain point, and your best man will present the rings. And any child-attendant issues can be cleared up at this time, as well. (Is the ringbearer, who is two years old, going to stay for the entire ceremony, or will he be shuffled out the back door by one of his parents at some point?)

The Recessional

Arm in arm, you and your new husband (or, for purposes of the rehearsal, *almost* new husband) lead the recessional, followed by your child attendants. Your maid of honor and best man are next, followed by your bridesmaids, who are paired with groomsmen as they walk out. The order of the Jewish recessional is as follows: bride and groom, bride's parents, groom's parents, child attendants, honor attendants, and bridesmaids paired with groomsmen. The cantor and rabbi walk at the end of the recessional.

The Rehearsal Dinner

The majority of wedding rehearsals are merely warm-ups for the truly important event of the evening: the rehearsal dinner and ensuing party. This celebration gives everyone involved in the wedding a chance to eat, drink, be merry, and finally relax and forget about the stresses of the big day to come. What this means is that your part in the planning is done. Leave the specifics of the wedding in the church. Everyone needs to let loose a little. Don't be a bossy bride and begrudge these people a nice evening.

REHEARSAL CHECKLIST WORKSHEET

Date and time of rehearsal:
....

○ Bride

○ Officiant

○ Maid of honor

○ Best man

○ Flower girl

○ Readings

○ Special blessings

○ Rings

○ Groom

○ Parents of bride and groom

○ Bridesmaids

○ Groomsmen

○ Ringbearer

○ Readers

○ Gift presenters

○ Marriage license

Additional information:
....

....

....

....

....

....

....

....

....

....

....

The Final Prewedding Party

The rehearsal dinner can be as formal or as informal as your host wants to make it. (However, it shouldn't be so formal as to run the risk of outdoing the wedding reception.) It can be held at someone's home, in a restaurant, in a park, on the beach—it can be anywhere. Dress accordingly.

Invitations can be extended by phone or by electronic invitation. There's no need to have special rehearsal dinner invitations printed up, unless you're just hankering to spend the money on them.

The Hosts and the Guests

Traditionally, the expense of the rehearsal party is borne by the groom's parents, but these days anyone who is up to the task can host the party. If you and your groom feel uncomfortable asking either set of parents to host this affair (and no one steps up to offer to play host in their places), go ahead and plan it yourselves.

Who should be invited? The absolute, bare-minimum guest list should include the following:

- All members of the wedding party, along with their spouses or significant others
- The parents of the bride and groom
- The ceremony officiant, along with his or her spouse
- Grandparents of the bride and groom

Of course, you can invite anyone else you want (with your hosts' okay), but try to keep the party on the intimate side. Remember, the goal of this party is to let everyone relax and to give you and your groom some additional time with loved ones who may only be in town for a few days.

Inviting out-of-town guests is a nice idea, too. You'll get to spend more time with people you probably don't see that often, and they'll feel that distance hasn't kept them from being a part of the festivities. They'll also appreciate the nice dinner and something to do instead of hanging out in their hotel rooms. Similarly, if you have close friends that you couldn't manage to fit into the wedding party, you can invite them, too.

One for You, and One for You . . .

The rehearsal dinner is usually when the bride and groom hand out their gifts to the attendants (and parents, perhaps). You might also choose to give your groom a wedding gift at this time, and he may have a little something wrapped up for you. However, if the two of you would rather hold off giving each other your wedding gifts until the honeymoon, that's not a horrible idea, especially if one or both of you is just too exhausted or nervous to appreciate another gift at this point. After all, each of you has put a lot of thought into the gift you've chosen. You want your groom to be able to take the time to really take note of the significance of what you've given him, and you want to be able to do the same with the gift he's giving to you.

Speech! Speech!

If you follow tradition, toasts will be a part of the evening. If the groom's parents are hosting, the father of the groom offers up a toast to the bride and groom and to the bride's parents. The father of the bride responds with a toast to the hosts and to the almost-newlyweds. The groom then toasts the bride and her family, and the bride responds with a toast to the groom and his family.

Of course, you're not being watched by the etiquette police, so if someone *else* wants to make a toast (or someone on that list of toasters would rather not speak publicly), you're not bound to follow the traditional order. And if you prefer to skip the toasts altogether, that's fine, too. Remember, there'll be enough formality on the day of the wedding.

REHEARSAL DINNER WORKSHEET

WEDDING REHEARSAL

Location:
....

Telephone:
....

Contact:
....

Date:
....

Time:
....

Directions:
....

....

Notes:
....

....

DINNER

Location:
....

Telephone:
....

Contact:
....

Date:
....

Time:
....

Directions:
....

....

Number of guests:
....

Menu:
....

....

Beverages:
....

....

Notes:
....

....

GUEST LIST FOR REHEARSAL DINNER WORKSHEET

Name:
....

Address:
....
....

Telephone:
....

◯ RSVP   Number in Party: _____
....

Name:
....

Address:
....
....

Telephone:
....

◯ RSVP   Number in Party: _____
....

Name:
....

Address:
....
....

Telephone:
....

◯ RSVP   Number in Party: _____
....

Name:
....

Address:
....
....

Telephone:
....

◯ RSVP   Number in Party: _____
....

Name:
....

Address:
....
....

Telephone:
....

◯ RSVP   Number in Party: _____
....

Name:
....

Address:
....
....

Telephone:
....

◯ RSVP   Number in Party: _____
....

Name:
....

Address:
....
....

Telephone:
....

◯ RSVP   Number in Party: _____
....

Name:
....

Address:
....
....

Telephone:
....

◯ RSVP   Number in Party: _____
....

Name:
....

Address:
....

....

Telephone:
....

◯ RSVP   Number in Party: ____
....

Name:
....

Address:
....

....

Telephone:
....

◯ RSVP   Number in Party: ____
....

Name:
....

Address:
....

....

Telephone:
....

◯ RSVP   Number in Party: ____
....

Name:
....

Address:
....

....

Telephone:
....

◯ RSVP   Number in Party: ____
....

Name:
....

Address:
....

....

Telephone:
....

◯ RSVP   Number in Party: ____
....

Name:
....

Address:
....

....

Telephone:
....

◯ RSVP   Number in Party: ____
....

Name:
....

Address:
....

....

Telephone:
....

◯ RSVP   Number in Party: ____
....

Name:
....

Address:
....

....

Telephone:
....

◯ RSVP   Number in Party: ____
....

CHAPTER 19

Your Honeymoon and Beyond

YOU'LL PROBABLY AGREE THAT, what with all the frenzied planning, coordinating, organizing, and worrying involved, getting married can feel like a full-time job—and then some. When it's all over with, you'll need more than just an ordinary vacation to recuperate. Your honeymoon is the perfect time to plan the vacation of your dreams.

Honeymoons for Every Budget

Ultimately, of course, your budget is likely to have at least as big an influence on your choice of destination as your dreams. Consult a travel agent or the Internet to find low-priced airfares, reduced-rate package deals, and other ways to save money. You may be pleasantly surprised. Perhaps you can afford a trip to Hawaii by staying at a less-than-four-star hotel, or travel Europe via hostels and off-the-beaten-path bed and breakfasts. Remember, however, to confirm that "inexpensive" lodging does not mean "without running water," "dilapidated," or "situated in the red-light district" (though all of these situations, in their own way, may add some excitement to your trip).

Tight-Budget Honeymoons

Some couples choose to postpone the trip for several months, either for financial reasons or because one partner just can't get the vacation time from work right after the wedding. But some couples who are on strict budgets are happy enough to just get away together, whether that means going camping, arranging for a low-cost visit to a friend's vacation home for the weekend, or taking a quick little jaunt to a city an hour away. There's no "right way" to honeymoon, and sometimes the more creative you have to get, the more romantic the trip can be. Bottom line: don't feel badly if you can't afford to tour the globe right after your wedding. You and your groom will have plenty of years of discovery ahead of you. Make the most of what you have right now.

If you're still in the early stages of planning your wedding and you just know that you won't be able to afford any sort of honeymoon, your travel agent might be able to help you by setting up a honeymoon registry (such as Honeyfund), where guests contribute to a trip instead of buying traditional wedding gifts like china or flatware.

Do You Need a Travel Agent?

In this day and age, the poor travel agent has fallen by the wayside, at least as far as the younger generation goes. Internet deals and instant access to airlines and hotels have made us ask why on earth we would ever enlist the help of someone else. In many cases, you can absolutely do the planning yourself, but there are some pitfalls to be aware of when planning a trip using the bargain travel sites. First, let's look at the benefits that travel agents can offer you.

Using Travel Agents

Maybe you scoff at the very idea of travel agents, reasoning that you can do all of this yourself, no problem! If you're going out of the country, however, you might benefit from working with an agent who can enlighten you as to the finer points of international travel. Because foreign vacations can get very complicated—with connecting flights that have to meet boats that have to meet trains—putting all the responsibility into the lap of a trained professional is a good idea.

First, your agent will be able to tell you which paperwork, identification, and other necessities you will need in order to travel abroad. Travel agents are also on the ball as far as alerting you to potential troubles. You might not want to travel to a certain spot because it is the rainy season. Or you might find out that your four-star resort will be adding another wing during your stay, which will mean a lot of around-the-clock noise. Nowadays, some foreign countries post travel alerts for Americans, which you'll want to know about before you attempt to board a plane to a restricted or dangerous area.

HONEYMOON BUDGET WORKSHEET

Item	Description	Projected Cost*	Actual Cost*	Balance Due
TRANSPORTATION				
Airfare				
Car rental				
Moped rental				
Bike rental				
Train pass				
Taxi				
Parking fees				
Other				
ACCOMMODATIONS				
Wedding night				
Honeymoon destination				
Other				
FOOD				
Meal plan				
Meals				
Drinks				
ENTERTAINMENT				
Souvenirs				
Spending money				
Tips				
Other				
TOTAL				

* including tax, if applicable

I Found the Deal by Myself!

Here's the deal when you book on sites such as Expedia or Orbitz: the vendors (hotels, car rental places, airlines) consider you a customer of the discount travel web company. As such, if a problem arises, you will be instructed to take it up with the web company, and that can be a time-consuming nightmare-and-a-half under ordinary conditions. On your honeymoon, it gets bumped up to triple-nightmare status.

Let's say you book a king-size suite in a four-star hotel in New York City. The pictures look great, and there's a promised continental breakfast each morning. When you arrive, you find the building is in obvious need of repair and cleaning; the continental breakfast amounts to a piece of toast and a cup of coffee; and worst of all, your suite has been given to another guest, leaving you with a much smaller (but equally pricey) room.

Complaining to management is likely to get you exactly nowhere. Even though hotels enter into agreements freely with bargain travel sites, they tend to not want to deal with guests who have booked rooms through them. And the dot-com companies themselves are not usually known for immediately rectifying bad experiences from guests who complain that they did not receive the goods that they were promised.

Bottom line on booking through bargain sites: buyer beware. Look for customer service promises and/or phone numbers that will allow you to talk to a human being if something goes wrong. Take the time to read the guest reviews on any hotel, car, or airline you're considering. Angry customers will take the time to give you the real skinny on the place; pleased customers will let you know that your trip will be just fine.

How and Where to Get Your Passports

Passports are relatively easy to obtain—but you'll need to start the process well in advance. Give yourself a minimum of six weeks, but you should really start as soon as you can to avoid any last-minute problems. It is possible to pay extra (somewhere in the range of an arm and a leg) for expedited service, which generally takes about two or three weeks.

Your first step is to fill out an application, which can be found online at www.state.gov/travel. If you're applying for the first time, you'll have to take the application to a passport agency or a passport acceptance facility. This isn't as hard as it sounds. Many of these facilities are located inside of the larger post offices, some libraries, and county offices. You'll need proof of U.S. citizenship (your birth certificate or naturalization certificate will do); a photo ID (such as a valid driver's license or government ID); two passport photos (which can be taken at many one-hour photo shops or drug stores); your Social Security card; and the money (as of this writing, the fee is $110 for a new passport book, and $30 for a passport card), plus another $25 in execution fees.

Travel Tips

If you're leaving town, as most honeymooners do, you may be entering foreign territory—literally or not. Even if you're not leaving the country but are visiting a place you've never been to, you might feel like a fish out of water. Here are some ways to prepare yourself for a great trip.

Do Your Homework

Before you take off on any vacation, you should acquaint yourself with the area you're traveling to. If you're going to

Chicago, for example, you won't need to rent a car, because public transportation is around every corner, and you'd never find a parking spot, anyway.

Know what kind of weather to expect. You're headed to the Caribbean, you say, and all you're going to need is a bikini and some sunscreen. But if you're vacationing during the hurricane season, you might want to bring a raincoat . . . and you might want to inquire about the resort's refund policy.

If you're headed to an all-inclusive resort, find out what that means, exactly. Have you paid for your lodging and food only? Are water sports and entertainment included? What about gratuities? Do you have to shell out money for transportation to and from the airport?

Educate Yourself More

If you're off to a foreign country, play the part of a diplomat. Learn some phrases in the native language. Don't expect everyone to speak English, and don't balk at the customs. If the food turns your stomach, don't chastise the locals for eating it. If the entire region seems to be less than sanitary, deal with it without causing an international incident. Remember, *you're* the foreigner here. Act as you would if you were a guest in someone's home, and you may just endear yourself to the locals.

You'll also want to research whether you'll need vaccinations before traveling abroad, and you should try to work in a physical and dental checkup before you take off, too. Get yourself a good travel guide for regions you'll be traveling through. Guidebooks are updated constantly and offer some of the best, most realistic information on foreign travel.

TRAVEL ARRANGEMENTS WORKSHEET

TRAVEL AGENCY

Name of travel agency:
....

Address:
....

Website:
....

Telephone:
....

Contact:
....

Hours:
....

Directions:
....

CAR RENTAL AGENCY

Name of car rental agency:
....

Address:
....

Website:
....

Telephone:
....

Contact:
....

Hours:
....

Description of reserved vehicle (make/model):
....

....

Terms:
....

TRANSPORTATION

Destination:
....

Carrier: Flight/Route:
....

Departure date: Time:
....

Arrival date: Time:
....

Confirmation number: Date:
....

Destination:

Carrier: .... Flight/Route:

Departure date: .... Time:

Arrival date: .... Time:

Confirmation number: .... Date:

ACCOMMODATIONS

Hotel:

Address:

Directions:

Website:

Telephone:

Check-in date: .... Time:

Check-out date: .... Time:

Type of room:

Daily rate: .... Total cost:

Confirmation number: .... Date:

Hotel:

Address:

Directions:

Website:

Telephone:

Check-in date: .... Time:

Check-out date: .... Time:

Type of room:

Daily rate: .... Total cost:

Confirmation number: .... Date:

Don't Forget . . .

It's actually safer to use your credit cards (or traveler's checks) than to carry around huge wads of cash. Call your credit card company in advance and let them know you'll be traveling. These days, companies are on high alert for credit card theft and fraud. If you live in Moline and someone is suddenly using your card in Venice, the company may put a hold on your account.

Of course, the regular budgeting stipulations apply. Don't go wild charging everything just because you're on vacation, and keep track of how much you're spending. Be aware that you will need some cash, however. If you're planning on hitting the smaller inns or restaurants in foreign countries, many of these establishments operate on a cash-only basis. Exchange your money for local currency before you leave, and have your groom wear a money belt for safekeeping.

Confirm your hotel reservations the week before you leave. There's nothing quite like dragging all your heavy luggage into a hotel lobby in some exotic locale, dreaming of a nice, long nap— only to find that you don't have a room and there's not a vacant room on the island. If the room you thought you booked isn't the room you're being given, speak up. Ask for the manager on duty, and don't take no for an answer.

Once you arrive at your hotel, don't be afraid to complain to the management if the services or accommodations are not to your satisfaction. And *don't* wait until you're leaving. Most reputable hotels will go out of their way to rectify any problems as soon as possible, whether that means having your room cleaned again (the right way) or moving you to another room that's not right next to the vending machines.

Settling in after the Honeymoon

Whether you've moved in together before the wedding or you're waiting until the ink is dry on the marriage license, learning to live with someone else can be a tough transition. If you're finding, suddenly, that your fiancé (or new husband) has some questionable hygiene rituals or that he is obsessive-compulsive about where the condiments can be placed in the refrigerator (they go on the door, not on the big shelves!), you might be wondering what the heck you've gotten yourself into. This is one thing that many newlyweds (or new roommates) don't talk about. To admit that the bloom is off the rose, so to speak, would be lessening your relationship in the eyes of others. You definitely don't want anyone to think that what you and your guy have is anything less than perfect, right?

You'd probably be surprised at how many of your friends feel the same way. One day, someone will admit to a little something (that her husband hogs the entire bed every night, for example, and that she doesn't find it the least bit endearing), and the floodgates will be opened. In the meantime, though . . . remember to be honest with your new spouse, and encourage him to be honest with you.